Beyond the profits system

About the author

HARRY SHUTT was educated at Oxford and Warwick universities. He worked for six years in the development and planning division of the Economist Intelligence Unit (EIU). He then moved to the research department of the General and Municipal Workers' Union (1973–76), and subsequently became chief economist at the Fund for Research and Investment for the Development of Africa (1977–79). Since then he has been an independent economic consultant. His books include *The Myth of Free Trade: Patterns of Protectionism Since 1945* (1985), *The Trouble with Capitalism: An Inquiry into the Causes of Global Economic Failure* (1998), *A New Democracy: Alternatives to a Bankrupt World Order* (2001) and *The Decline of Capitalism: Can a Self-Regulated Profits System Survive?* (2005).

Also available from Zed Books

The Trouble with Capitalism: An Inquiry into the Causes of Global Economic Failure
A New Democracy: Alternatives to a Bankrupt World Order
The Decline of Capitalism: Can a Self-Regulated Profits System Survive?

Beyond the profits system

Possibilities for a post-capitalist era

HARRY SHUTT

Fernwood Publishing
HALIFAX & WINNIPEG

Zed Books
LONDON & NEW YORK

Beyond the Profits System: Possibilities for a Post-capitalist Era
was first published in 2010

Published in Canada by Fernwood Publishing Ltd,
32 Oceanvista Lane, Black Point, Nova Scotia BOJ 1BO
www.fernwoodpublishing.ca

Published in the rest of the world by
Zed Books Ltd, 7 Cynthia Street, London N1 9JF, UK
and Room 400, 175 Fifth Avenue, New York, NY 10010, USA
www.zedbooks.co.uk

FSC
Mixed Sources
Product group from well-managed
forests and other controlled sources
Cert no. SGS-COC-002953
www.fsc.org
© 1996 Forest Stewardship Council

Designed and typeset in Monotype Jansen
by illuminati, Grosmont
Cover designed by Rogue Four Design
Printed and bound in the UK by CPI Antony Rowe,
Chippenham and Eastbourne

Distributed in the USA exclusively by Palgrave Macmillan, a division
of St Martin's Press, LLC, 175 Fifth Avenue, New York, NY 10010, USA

A catalogue record for this book is available from the British Library
Library of Congress Cataloging in Publication Data available
Library and Archives Canada Cataloguing in Publication
Shutt, Harry
    Beyond the profits system : possibilities for a post-capitalist
era / Harry Shutt.
ISBN 978-1-55266-359-2
    1. Economics.   2. Economic history—21st century.   3. Capitalism.
I. Title.
HC51.S493 2010   330.9   C2010-900700-X

ISBN 978 1 84813 416 4 Hb (Zed)
ISBN 978 1 84813 417 1 Pb (Zed)
ISBN 978 1 84813 418 8 Eb (Zed)
ISBN 978 1 55266 359 2 (Fernwood)

Contents

Introduction

Two years on from the start of the 'credit crunch' which has precipitated the sharpest fall in global economic activity since the 1930s, a striking air of unreality pervades public discussion of the appropriate response to it. Thus most mainstream economists focus on the merits of rival policy prescriptions – giving greater or lesser weight to different forms of fiscal or monetary stimulus (including some which would until recently have been dismissed as a recipe for disaster) – while often conceding that they have no idea whether or when their proposed remedies will succeed in restoring equilibrium. What all have in common, however, is a professed belief that sooner or later recovery will somehow occur and that the capitalist system – based on the pursuit of private profit maximisation – will be restored to health.

Such apparent complacency is in striking contrast to the position that prevailed in comparable circumstances in the 1930s. At that time the global devastation which stemmed from the Wall Street Crash of 1929 led many to look to the Communist model of the newly established Soviet Union as a more rational alternative to the catastrophically failed model of Western capitalism. For there was no denying Soviet success in maintaining expansion and full employment in the 1930s – in isolation from the paralysed economies of the West – even if few were then aware of the horrific human cost that was also involved.

Now, some eighty years later, in the midst of a comparable economic upheaval, there is no sign of any alternative model being proposed by any political movement or pressure group of significance in the industrialised world. Following the collapse of the Soviet system at the end of the 1980s nearly all the world's Communist and former Communist countries, including China, have effectively been drawn into the orbit of the global capitalist economy, with which they seem destined to sink or swim. Elsewhere the deprived masses of the Third World are variously subjected to obscurantist calls for a return to Islamic fundamentalist values or to long discredited Maoist slogans, while seemingly more coherent models of development adopted by Venezuela and other Latin American countries face the unremitting hostility of the free-market ideologues in Washington and consequent marginalisation by the international community of aid donors.

Hence it may be said that there now exists a glaring ideological vacuum in a world whose leaders still insist that, as proclaimed by British prime minister Margaret Thatcher in the 1980s, 'there is no alternative' to the model of liberalised market capitalism which has held global sway for the last thirty years. Indeed it is a remarkable and seemingly inexplicable fact that what we may term the global establishment has succeeded in maintaining such uniform political commitment to this model for so long. For there have been many signs over the years of increasing fragility in the global financial and economic order – including the world-wide stock-market crashes of 1987 and 2000 and a number of localised crises affecting Mexico, East Asia and Russia in the 1990s – as well as mounting symptoms of social distress and consequent discontent and disorder across the world.

Whatever the reason for the failure of any serious opposition to this manifestly flawed ideology to appear – based on a reasoned alternative – the time is long overdue for a broad and open public debate on the kind of radically different model that is desperately needed. It is with a view to contributing to such a debate that the present work has been written. Its purpose may be summarised as twofold:

- to demonstrate why present official policies intended to promote early revival of the global economy are bound to fail and why no model dependent on perpetuating growth and the maximisation of private profit can be sustainable in future;
- to outline the principles on which a more economically stable and socially tolerable order could be based.

Readers may be struck by the fact that much of the analysis and ideas set out in the book are far from new – and indeed have a pedigree dating from the early days of the Industrial Revolution in the nineteenth century. In fact, the continuing relevance of the critique of Marx, Engels, Carlyle, Ruskin, Morris and others of the ideology of industrial capitalism – from a sociological, cultural and even moral perspective as well as an economic one – may be seen as a powerful testament both to the system's enduring destructiveness and to the tenacity of its supporters in resisting all attempts to tame it. The clear lesson is that it will be no mean task to overcome the entrenched forces of resistance to fundamental change.

If the circumstances of the present crisis nevertheless give hope that it may now be possible to envisage an early transition to a less dysfunctional economic and social order, it is because:

1. the inherent tension between the need for the capitalist economy to generate an ever greater level of profit for investors and the need for the rest of society to appropriate a large enough share of value-added – gross domestic product (GDP) – in order to meet the basic needs of the wider public for adequate income and public services (and other socially desirable purposes) has now reached a political breaking point;

2. technological change has rendered capitalism obsolete, given that the need to assemble large amounts of investment capital in order to meet the demands of the new mechanical age ushered in some two hundred years ago by the development of steam power (which, as Marx and Engels pointed out, made necessary the transition from feudalism to capitalism[1]) has now disappeared as the digital age heralds an end to society's need for such large-scale capital investment – and hence for the profits demanded by private investors.

To any readers who feel the lack of a more detailed analysis of why and how the modern capitalist profits system[2] has become so dysfunctional and unworkable, it is respectfully suggested that they refer to the author's earlier books, in particular *The Trouble with Capitalism* (1998) and *The Decline of Capitalism* (2005). In the modest belief that the analysis and predictions of those works have been substantially vindicated – even if predictably ignored by more mainstream commentators – it seems appropriate to conclude that the time for further in-depth analysis of how we arrived at the present point of breakdown is now past, and that attention should rather be concentrated on the urgent task of building a survivable future.

---

1. *Manifesto of the Communist Party* (1848).
2. The terms 'capitalism' and 'profits system' are used interchangeably in this book; a preference for the latter is based on the view that it better expresses the essential weakness of the system, particularly in the contemporary context.

I

Anatomy of a crisis

THE GLOBAL FINANCIAL and economic crisis which began in
2007 has unquestionably been the most severe to have af-
flicted the world economy since that of 1929–33. The latter marked
the start of the Great Depression of the 1930s – a disaster which
was only finally ended by the stimulus of massive destruction and
armaments production induced by World War II. The huge scale
of wealth and livelihood destruction caused by the present disaster
– which is ongoing at the time of writing (summer 2009) – is
reflected in the fact that the market capitalisation of the world's
major stock exchanges fell by 47 per cent in value (a loss of $29.4
trillion – equal to about half of global GDP) in the twelve months
to December 2008.[1] To put this in perspective, the proportionate
scale of loss not only dwarfed that in any previous calendar year
on record (at least since World War II) but compares with a net
decline of only 35 per cent over the whole of the previous market
collapse (from end 1999 to end 2002).

---

1. World Federation of Exchanges, www.world-exchanges.org. The data cover
all the world's major exchanges except Moscow.

5

One of the most striking phenomena of the unfolding crisis has been the uniformly superficial nature of the analysis of its causes presented by mainstream observers, whether government officials, academics or business representatives. Thus it is commonly stated that the crisis was caused by a combination of imprudent investment by bankers and others (often incentivised by reward structures appealing to extreme greed) and unduly lax official regulation and supervision of markets. Yet the obvious question begged by such explanations – of how or why such a dysfunctional climate came to be created – is never addressed in any serious fashion. This omission is all the more remarkable when it is well known, for example, that

- the US Glass–Steagall Act – enacted in 1933 in order to outlaw many of the conflicts of interest and excesses in the financial markets that had led to the Wall Street crash of 1929 – was repealed in 1999 by the Clinton administration with bipartisan support in Congress, thereby facilitating a reprise of the more or less criminal practices of seventy years earlier and thus contributing greatly to the present financial market implosion;
- the Commodity Futures Modernization Act of 2000 – also enacted by President Clinton with strong Republican support – legalised forms of speculation (in commodities and financial derivatives such as credit default swaps – see below) that were previously classified as illegal gambling.[2]

The inescapable conclusion, therefore, is that the crisis was the product of a conscious process of facilitating ever greater risk of massive systemic failure. At the same time, given the competitive, profit-maximising climate in which financial institutions are

---

2. Joshua Holland, '"American Casino": How Our Nation's Financial Sector Became a Massive and Unregulated Gambling Operation', *Alternet*, 5 September 2009, www.alternet.org/story/142267.

operating, and the creation of incentive and reward structures encouraging the pursuit of short-term gain at all costs – individual agents effectively had no choice but to exploit every loophole to push risk-taking to the limit of what was allowed – and often beyond it.

Moreover, the power of the vested interests behind this compulsion has been revealed by the lack of will on the part of regulators such as the Securities Exchange Commission in the USA and the Bank of England and Financial Services Authority in Britain to enforce those rules that remained in force – such as the laws against fraud.[3] Given the obvious culpability of the ruling establishment revealed by this line of enquiry it is perhaps only too unremarkable that mainstream analysts do not wish to pursue it – all the more so as it serves to highlight the fundamental unacceptability of a system dependent on sustaining impossibly high levels of economic growth.

If this anarchic situation was deliberately contrived, one might suppose that those now ostensibly seeking ways to order affairs better in future would try to discover why such a high-risk policy has been consciously pursued. To this question there can be only one plausible answer (which obviously cannot be spoken in mainstream circles): the compulsion to find ever more outlets for the rising volume of investible funds generated by the inexorable expansion of accumulated profits as the global economy has continued to grow over the years (albeit at a progressively slower rate from the 1970s).[4] This in turn points to a recognition (if only unconscious) on the part of the ruling establishment that

3. Notably in the case of the huge Madoff 'Ponzi' fraud in the USA and the (so far) much less reported case of systematic mortgage fraud (encouragement of borrowers to 'self-certify' their incomes as much higher than they actually were) in Britain.

4. See Harry Shutt, *The Trouble with Capitalism: An Enquiry into the Causes of Global Economic Failure* (London: Zed Books, 1998), chs 6, 7 and 8.

the historic source of capitalist instability – the business cycle of boom and bust, linked to the phenomenon of the falling rate of profit, first identified by Karl Marx – was reasserting itself.

Consistent with their general reluctance to apportion blame, there has been little attempt in establishment circles to expose the serial dishonesty of such key officials as Alan Greenspan, chairman of the US Federal Reserve Board, 1987–2006. The latter, having famously warned of the 'irrational exuberance' of stock-market investors as prices on Wall Street soared in late 1996, nevertheless sought to justify them in 1999 at levels which by then had doubled again, on the manifestly spurious grounds that rapidly rising productivity in the USA meant that they were indefinitely sustainable – even though such a consideration was at best irrelevant, bearing in mind that weak demand in a slowing world economy was a decisively negative factor of far greater significance. Linked to this argument, the chairman also gave his blessing to the view that the so-called New Economy – based on the wonders of electronics, cyber-technology and enhanced telecommunications – could somehow provide the basis for sustained rapid growth. When shortly afterwards the related 'dotcom' bubble burst with disastrous consequences for the markets, Greenspan and his colleagues at the Fed proceeded to cut interest rates to 1 per cent in a determined and successful attempt to generate a speculative revival in asset prices. When this resulted in a manifestly unsustainable real-estate bubble, whose collapse in 2007 (after Greenspan had left office) was to be the catalyst of the present crisis, he quite falsely claimed throughout that it was impossible to identify the existence of such bubbles until after they had burst. So far from denouncing this systematic falsehood and betrayal of the public interest, politicians of both Republican and Democratic parties for years uniformly lauded Greenspan as a 'national treasure' and indispensable guarantor of economic prosperity.

The roots of disaster

In truth this tendency of the global establishment to engage in escapist fantasy may be considered understandable in view of the political realities that had become established after World War II. For it was a political article of faith for long after the war that Western governments – at least in the industrialised countries – could and should manage their economies so as to maintain more or less full employment[5] most of the time, given the consensus that high unemployment was an unacceptable social scourge which had helped create the conditions leading to war. This objective was to be attained by a combination of (a) manipulating the level of economic activity through fiscal and monetary policy so as to sustain high rates of GDP growth (in line with Keynesian principles) and (b) selective state intervention to support different sectors through subsidies of one form or another. As a result any downturns could, it was believed, be kept mild and short-lived enough to avoid any serious social hardship, especially as the countervailing presence of the welfare state (also seen as indispensable by all political parties) would be able to mitigate any transient social damage. Small wonder that the apparent success of this 'mixed economy' model of economic management in delivering high rates of growth and rising prosperity for nearly everyone in the industrialised world over the twenty-five years after the war convinced many that the capitalist system's susceptibility to the business cycle had at last been permanently cured.

Against this background it was naturally hard for many, including the political establishment, to come to terms with the sudden onset of recession in 1974. (Even more disconcertingly, this downturn was accompanied by the highest rates of inflation

---

5. This very loosely defined concept was then generally felt to be compatible with a rate of unemployment no higher than 3–4 per cent of the workforce.

experienced since World War I – something which economists had always been taught to believe could not happen while the economy was contracting.) For the reality revealed by this crisis was that the mixed-economy model was unable after all to deliver perpetual growth, as its champions had insisted, and indeed could not prevent the return of the business cycle. (With hindsight it may plausibly be concluded that the prolonged post-war boom had in any case owed far more to the stimulus of post-war reconstruction and pent-up consumer demand – which had been so constrained by recession and war for a decade and a half up to 1945 – than to the impact of 'demand management' policies.)

In face of this shock to the post-war consensus, all mainstream political parties and interest groups were agreed that the priority must be to restore and maintain the high rates of growth on which post-war prosperity had been built. Yet a strong difference of opinion emerged between those who, clinging to Keynesian orthodoxy, maintained that all that was required was further intervention in the market to control prices and incomes (thus limiting inflation) and those who claimed that what was needed instead was to remove government controls on markets and place reliance on monetary policy alone (in practice influenced solely through adjustment in interest rates) to maintain price stability. This so-called monetarist approach, which its advocates maintained would promote prosperity by 'unleashing the forces of enterprise', was soon to prevail and has remained dominant ever since, being identified successively with the political agenda of the administrations of Prime Minister Thatcher in Britain and President Reagan in the USA, which came to power in 1979 and 1981 respectively – but has since become more commonly referred to as neoliberalism.

While this change of emphasis was presented by many of its supporters as a 'revolution', to a large extent its radicalism was more apparent then real. For in one crucial respect even the most vocal enthusiasts for 'rolling back the frontiers of the state' accepted, indeed insisted, that no fundamental change in the mixed-economy model was to be contemplated. This was the continued judicious deployment of public-sector resources – particularly through tax breaks and other more direct forms of subsidy – to encourage private-sector interests and prop up their profits. Indeed a central tenet of the Reagan administration's policy was the belief that cutting taxes of the wealthy and the corporate sector would so arouse their enterprising 'animal spirits' as to generate a major expansion of investment and output, thereby offsetting the initial loss of government revenue resulting from the tax cuts. In truth, as a number of commentators pointed out at the time, this amounted to a form of Keynesian fiscal stimulus such as the Reaganite neoliberals claimed had been discredited.[6] Meanwhile there was also a massive increase in those areas of public spending of benefit to the private sector – notably the armaments industry, which was disproportionately well represented in the Reagan cabinet. As against this, however, social welfare benefits and entitlements were successively curtailed, as also by the Thatcher regime in Britain, even if their total budgetary cost was not contained as the number of claimants grew in the wake of rising unemployment in the 1980s.[7]

But while the socially regressive nature of these neoliberal strategies was perhaps the feature that excited greatest hostility from their opponents in the 1980s, their most serious failing was one that has gone largely unnoticed both then and subsequently: their inability to achieve any sustained revival of growth – not

6. J.K. Galbraith, *The World Economy since the War: A Personal View* (London: Mandarin, 1995).

7. John O'Connor, 'US Social Welfare Policy: The Reagan Record and Legacy', *Cambridge Journal of Social Policy*, January 1998.

to mention the steep rise in public deficits and indebtedness stemming from the tax cuts. In fact, it should have been clear already by the time of the stock-market 'crash' of October 1987 – and certainly by its inflationary aftermath in the bursting of the banking and real-estate bubbles of 1989–90 – that the neoliberal model offered no better antidote to the recurrence of the business cycle than the Keynesian mixed-economy model. Thus annual GDP growth of the industrialised countries of around 3.5 per cent on average in the 1970s (accounting for around 80 per cent of global output) – already viewed as inadequate in comparison to the much higher rates achieved in the 1960s – actually declined further thereafter, to around 2.8 per cent in the 1980s and 2.5 per cent in the 1990s.[8]

Thus, taking the post-World War II period as a whole, it may be concluded that the central failure of policy has been the ultimate inability to escape from the business cycle or neutralise its impact. This has not been for want of trying. For in tandem with official policies of 'demand management' the business community has been devoted, as never before, to stimulating and expanding consumer demand in what may be seen as the classic era of marketing and advertising (see Chapter 5). Likewise the attempt to sustain consumption growth has also been reinforced by the progressive relaxation of laws restricting such morally questionable activities as pornography and gambling[9] (though strangely not the use of narcotics – see Chapter 4), thereby extending the scope of consumer markets. In the same spirit, the whole realm of sport has become fully commercialised since World War II, to the point where the Olympic Games – for long a purely amateur competition in line with its founding precepts – has become as professionalised, fiercely competitive and dominated by com-

8. OECD, *National Accounts Statistics*; IMF, *World Economic Outlook*.
9. See Shutt, *The Trouble with Capitalism*, ch. 3.

mercial interests as any major sporting event, complete with the ubiquitous taint of performance-enhancing substances. That this effort has nonetheless ended in failure may be ascribed not only to the inevitable saturation of markets – familiar from earlier business cycles – but also to a steadily growing resistance to 'consumerism' among sections of the public in the industrialised world (see Chapter 3).

This failure, it may be argued, was compounded by another crucial negative influence in the long-term evolution of capitalism that seems to have become more pronounced by the 1980s. This was the continuing long-term trend towards a decline in the growth of fixed capital investment (as a proportion of GDP in industrialised countries) which had set in since the end of the 1960s.[10] There seems little doubt that this trend was largely a function of the falling capital intensity of production as a result of changing technology – and also of a shift in the pattern of consumer demand away from manufactures in favour of less capital-intensive services, which is an observable function of the rise in real personal incomes over time.[11] At all events the resulting glut of capital looking for outlets for reinvestment – such as is always being generated as the 'surplus value' of the profits system – posed immense strain on global capitalism. Indeed, as capital became more of a super-abundant rather than a scarce factor of production there was increasingly a perverse incentive to utilise more of it rather than less – especially in situations of quasi-monopoly where the incentive to cost-effectiveness was blunted (see Chapter 4).

---

10. Shutt, *The Trouble with Capitalism*, pp. 55–9.

11. It is notable that the phenomenon of diminishing capital intensity of production and the consequent reduced demand for it was observable from the 1970s, although the dominant vested interests have resolutely refused to recognise this. See André Gorz, *Farewell to the Working Class* (London: Pluto Press, 1982); Shutt, *The Trouble with Capitalism*, p. 98.

A related phenomenon of great significance in the evolution of economic strategies in the neoliberal era was the declining demand for labour – relative both to its supply and to the level of output. This was clearly the result of both the slowing overall growth of output and the same technological change that was tending to depress the demand for capital. Yet just as the authorities could not bring themselves explicitly to recognise the inescapable economic trends leading to the devaluation of capital, neither could they publicly acknowledge that the market for labour was similarly affected. This was because to do so would have meant taking steps to modify income distribution structures so as to assure greater social equality – whether through enhanced transfer payments by means of taxation and social protection schemes or through effective rationing of employment opportunities via reductions in working hours. More fundamentally, it would have entailed giving up the crucial ability of capitalist enterprises to exploit labour by driving down wages so as to enhance profit levels. Hence governments have found it necessary to continue pretending that unemployment is not a serious problem – mainly through statistical sleight of hand (changing definitions and targets) – and by the same token that full employment is perfectly attainable. Yet the reality is reflected in indicators that are harder to distort, notably the level of average wages, which in the USA (for example) fell by almost 20 per cent in real terms between 1974 and 1994.

Speculative folly

It was undoubtedly the deepening imbalance in the demand for and supply of investment capital which lay behind some novel features of the 1980s' global economy that may be seen as the consequence of the ever-widening search for new outlets for it. Among these were the increasing vogue for privatisation of public utilities and other state-owned assets, mergers and acquisitions of private-sector companies and public-sector debt (the supply of which was greatly expanded as a result of rising fiscal deficits, notably in the United States as the Reagan administration's tax cuts failed to achieve the promised stimulus to growth). At the same time there was a quite surprising trend towards investing in higher risk assets, such as securities in 'emerging' markets (previously considered off-limits for all but the most expert – or foolhardy – investors) or 'junk' bonds (issued by companies with low credit ratings and therefore offering higher yields). An important feature of much of this investment was its increasingly speculative character – that is to say it was based on buying at least as much with a view to appreciation in the market value of the assets as for the prospective dividend or interest yield.[12] This was reflected in the steep rise in the market valuation of company shares – relative to earnings – after 1980 to something like double the historic ratio by the time the dotcom bubble burst in 2000, and in the corresponding decline of dividend yields.[13] Given that this prolonged bull market in equities occurred at a time when, as we have seen, global growth rates recorded a long-term downward trend, it should have been obvious long before the bubble burst that market valuations were being excessively inflated as a result of the 'irrational exuberance' identified by Chairman Greenspan himself in 1996. So far from this, however, Wall Street analysts continued up to 2000 to project corporate earnings growth of 8–10 per cent a year indefinitely, despite real GDP growth rates of no more than 2–3 per cent. In such circumstances it was obvious

12. See Shutt, *The Trouble with Capitalism*, chs 6, 7 and 8.

13. As reflected in data from the Standard & Poor's 500 index, widely considered the most representative benchmark of the US stock market. This is broadly in line with the pattern in other OECD stock markets, although not Japan, where prices collapsed sharply in 1990 from an all-time high to levels which have never subsequently exceeded half that peak.

that market valuations were building up to an inevitable massive correction. By the same token it was equally clear that the market value of most stocks could only be kept moving upwards on the basis of increasingly fraudulent 'hype' as to their earnings potential.

The temptation to engage in such fraud was greatly enhanced by the process of deregulation and liberalisation of the financial sector and markets which was one of the defining tendencies of the neoliberal era ushered in by the Reagan and Thatcher regimes. The most significant features of this process were

1. removal of all restrictions on cross-border capital movements (also involving total freedom of currency exchange);
2. banks were enabled significantly to expand their balance sheets by allowing them to include a broader range of assets (including some securities) in their regulated capital base, while at the same time 'levering up' – that is, lending an ever higher multiple of this base figure;
3. companies were enabled to buy back their own shares – a practice that had long been effectively outlawed in most countries, precisely to prevent them from manipulating their own share prices, which they now proceeded to do;
4. different financial services (deposit-taking and both trading and underwriting of securities) could be combined in the same group, thus creating the potential for significant conflicts of interest and incentives for excessive risk-taking.

The combined effect of these changes was to create the conditions for a rapid expansion of credit without central banks or other regulatory authorities being able to control it – other than through the manipulation of interest rates. Underpinning this ever more freewheeling structure of finance was the implicit understanding that the state (in its historic role as 'lender of last resort') could be called on to bail out any institution that got into serious difficulties, at least if it was large enough for its collapse to threaten the stability of the entire financial system. Hence despite the official claim that the rewards of highly paid bankers, fund managers and speculators were appropriate compensation for the risks they were taking, in reality most of the institutions they worked for enjoyed the ultimate protection of the taxpayer. The obvious temptation to take excessive risks provided by this implicit indemnity against their own failings is commonly referred to as a state of 'moral hazard'. This was to become an ever more dominant influence from the 1980s, although its significance was naturally little emphasised by those benefiting from it.

A further pernicious element in the dangerously permissive environment thus being created under the neoliberal banner was what has come to be known as globalisation. This essentially meant that the principle of maximum deregulation was extended across international borders, mainly through removal of restrictions on movements of capital as well as goods and services. This inevitably created conditions in which individual countries found it hard to impose strict controls or anything more than minimal taxes on corporations or investors who could easily move their businesses to countries where they might expect to get more favourable treatment. The fear of being thus blackmailed by private investors naturally led countries to engage in a competitive lowering of tax rates and of standards governing financial regulation – not to mention treatment of labour and the environment. At the same time financial institutions and investors have been able to exploit the varying national standards of market regulation to play the game of 'regulatory arbitrage', thereby intensifying the destructive anarchy of the financial markets. Despite the widespread evidence of the damage wrought by this 'race to the bottom' (particularly among the poorest and most disadvantaged countries) the global establishment has sustained a virtually unanimous chorus of praise for it since the 1980s – notwithstanding warnings from within the Organisation for Economic Co-operation and Development (OECD)[14] itself since the 1990s of the dangers arising from unbridled 'tax competition' among governments.[15]

The growing speculative element in the pattern of investment from the 1980s had other momentous consequences for the evolution of financial markets. For just as such speculation was a consequence of the generation of excess investible funds through the normal development of the capitalist business cycle, so it was also necessary – in order to support the more or less continuous rise in the market value of assets – to facilitate a continuously expanding flow of funds into the market. Thus, paradoxically, the cyclical excess of capital arising from profit generation could only be prevented from bringing about a market crash of the traditional kind – with all the politically intolerable destruction of wealth and livelihoods that would have entailed – by introducing even greater inflows of funds to underpin their market value.

In the USA and other market economies this process had been facilitated at least since the 1960s by the institutionalised flow of savings (attracted by tax breaks) into mutual, pension and other retirement funds, which were then deployed in the markets. Naturally the thoroughgoing liberalisation of financial markets initiated in the 1980s was designed to magnify this 'wall of money' still further. Yet given that this artificial stimulation of fund flows was obviously tending to cause an even greater imbalance between the excess of investible funds and the demand for productive investment of such funds, the inevitable consequence was an ever stronger propensity to speculative investment.

---

14. The 'club' of industrialised market economy countries.
15. *Harmful Tax Competition: An Emerging Global Issue* (OECD 1998).

A notable symptom of the growing importance of pure speculation, rather than facilitation of productive investment, in the
securities markets has been the emergence of financial institutions dedicated almost exclusively to exploiting the speculative
opportunities created in the newly liberalised markets. These
comprise

1. *hedge funds* – to which wealthy investors are prepared to pay
   very large fees in return for the high growth they purport to
   achieve (and often did during the boom) through short-term
   'arbitrage' (speculative buying and selling) of assets of all
   kinds;
2. *private equity institutions* – which attract investors to place their
   money (usually for longer periods and in larger quantities than
   in the case of hedge funds) on the basis that it will be used to
   acquire whole public companies which are deemed to be under-
   valued, with a view to restructuring them as private companies
   (thus removed from the scrutiny of the public exchanges) and
   then disposing of them again via a sale or market flotation
   at a large profit. This process generally involves replacing a
   significant portion of equity on the balance sheet with higher
   levels of debt, thereby enabling the private equity partners
   to extract large amounts of shareholder value for themselves
   – which may be described as de facto asset stripping – while
   leaving the restructured company with higher fixed costs and
   potentially under greater financial pressure than before (see
   also Chapter 4).

While these institutions have sought to justify their activities
in terms of their ability to help eliminate inefficiencies in the
market valuation of assets and in the management of companies,
it may be doubted whether they would exist at all but for the
ever growing glut of speculative capital searching desperately for

profitable outlets. As such they have come to be widely perceived as a source of market and corporate destabilisation – producing fabulous rewards for a few at the expense of the many – and have been popularly referred to by German politicians as 'locusts'.[16]

The descent into criminality

Inevitably in this climate of reduced growth and diminished scope for sustaining profitability the combined pressures of intensifying competition and officially sanctified incentives to take ever greater risks meant there was a temptation for market players to bend the rules progressively further in pursuit of the huge financial rewards on offer. This was dramatically demonstrated in the wake of the bursting of the dotcom bubble in 2000, when systematic deception on the part of Wall Street analysts and share traders came to light and the largest corporate fraud in US history – involving the Enron corporation and its auditors, Arthur Andersen – was exposed.

Following this, attempts were made to tighten the law and regulatory framework in the USA, notably by the Sarbanes–Oxley Act of 2002, which made company chief executives criminally liable in person for any false accounts lodged by their companies. However, the financial meltdown from 2007 – leading to the belated exposure of the massive fraud perpetrated by Bernard Madoff and other operators of financial pyramid (or Ponzi) schemes[17] – has shown how little deterrent effect such measures have had. More alarmingly still, they appear to have revealed how easy it had become for well-connected financiers to persuade regulators

---

16. The term coined by former vice-chancellor Franz Müntefering.

17. Schemes where existing investors' returns and redemptions are paid out of funds subscribed by new investors rather than from the investment income of the fund itself, enabling the fund operators to divert funds to their own private purposes as long as the inflow of new investments is sustained.

such as the Securities and Exchange Commission (SEC) to turn a blind eye to blatant evidence of wrongdoing. Likewise even more mainstream US companies, which have been forced to own up by the SEC to cooking the books in their desperate efforts to 'make the numbers' expected by the markets, have been able to escape the kind of punishment that would have been indicated by the Sarbanes–Oxley Act and simply, as in the past, pay a fine without admitting wrongdoing.

Yet an even greater fraud inflicted on the financial sector – which has nevertheless received the official blessing of regulators such as former Fed chairman Greenspan – has been the mushrooming tide of securities generically known under the heading of structured finance. These refer to both

1. financial 'derivatives', including risk hedging products such as credit default swaps (CDS), whose avowed purpose is to make it possible for anyone to insure against the possibility of any default by issuers of debt; and
2. asset-backed securities (ABSs)/collateralised debt obligations (CDOs) – by which loans (particularly mortgages) were 'repackaged' into securities and sold on to investors, with a view to spreading any risk among many 'counterparties' on the basis that the cost of default for any one of them would thereby be minimised.

The reason for describing these instruments as essentially fraudulent is that they were evidently designed to be at once so complex that they were extremely difficult to value based on the fundamentals of the underlying assets[18] and at the same time were traded mainly on a non-transparent, 'over-the-counter' basis (i.e. away from any public exchanges) so that any market-based

---

18. Satyajit Das, 'How to Design Derivatives that Dazzle and Obfuscate', *Financial Times*, 8 July 2009.

valuation was virtually impossible. Despite this obvious opacity there has been well-financed, highly effective lobbying to foil any attempts to submit them to official regulation. Instead investors were forced to rely on credit ratings provided by members of the de facto cartel of ratings agencies,[19] who routinely awarded the highest rating (triple-A) to these securities, for which they were paid by the issuers themselves – a blatant, but until recently little remarked, conflict of interest. This combination of complexity, obfuscation and de facto corruption is obviously consistent with an intention deliberately to deceive investors.

Because of the lack of any central exchange or regulatory oversight there is no reliable information as to the size of these markets or control over the creditworthiness of the investors or counterparties involved. The dangers posed by this situation are apparent from the fact that the value of global CDS contracts was unofficially estimated at no less than $45–65 *trillion* in early 2009. Since this amount is approximately equal to aggregate global GDP it is safe to assume that the vast majority of these contracts were purely speculative bets rather than transactions for the purpose of genuine insurance against default.[20] Already by that time the exposure of the US insurance giant AIG to a mere $1.6 trillion on which it was unable to honour its commitments in September 2008 was enough to bring it to its knees and force the US government effectively to nationalise it in order to avert total market collapse. Nothing could illustrate better the deadly consequences of combining unregulated markets with the moral hazard of an implicit state guarantee. Moreover, huge volumes of such 'toxic waste' – particularly of ABSs and CDOs based on sub-prime mortgages – are now weighing down the balance sheets of many

---

19. Standard & Poor's, Moody's & Fitch.
20. It has been unofficially estimated that some 80 per cent of these transactions were purely speculative.

other major financial institutions, which are consequently also in need of taxpayer support. (Again the problem is compounded by the fact that the market value of the securities – relative to their book value – is uncertain, albeit certainly much lower, in the absence of an exchange where they can be traded.)

An additionally pernicious feature of CDSs – which have been described by Warren Buffett, the most celebrated living American investor, as 'financial weapons of mass destruction' – is that they can create an opportunity and incentive for speculative investors to try to force companies on which they hold them into default, as allegedly happened in 2009 in the case of a bank in Kazakhstan on which the leading finance house Morgan Stanley held a large CDS position which was supposed to pay out when it called in a loan, pushing the bank into default.[21] Despite this and the havoc wrought by AIG's CDS losses – leading to attempts in the US House of Representatives to legislate to ban these instruments outright – the Obama administration has (as of summer 2009) done no more than pay lip-service to the need to subject them to greater transparency. In this context it is pertinent to recall that under the Clinton administration ten years earlier there was not only powerful resistance to any attempt to regulate the derivatives market – led by Treasury Secretary Lawrence Summers, since January 2009 director of the National Economic Council for President Barack Obama, and Fed chairman Greenspan – but that new legislation was enacted to deregulate it further[22] (see above).

In the final analysis this apparent moral degeneracy has to be seen as the inevitable consequence of trying to evade the inescapable logic of the capitalist business cycle: the survival of

---

21. Gillian Tett, 'Tale from the Land of Borat is a Lesson to the World at Large', *Financial Times*, 1 May 2009.

22. Anthony Faiola, Ellen Nakashima and Jill Drew, 'What Went Wrong', *Washington Post*, 15 October 2008.

the profits system could only be assured by accepting periodic bouts of destruction which are no longer politically tolerable. Since the alternative of trying to develop a radically different and less destructive model of economic organisation was considered equally unacceptable by the dominant elite, the perception gradually developed that preserving the status quo was an end that could justify almost any means.

The political nexus

Another crucial element driving this slide towards ever more irresponsible and criminal conduct in the financial community has been the huge political power of big business as a whole, exercised (most obviously in the USA) through campaign contributions to elected officials. Its ability to exercise this profoundly anti-democratic power has naturally been consolidated by its effective domination of the media and, increasingly, also such opinion-forming channels as the universities. This has been blatantly reflected in hitherto largely successful lobbying campaigns: against attempts to subject such opaque areas of the financial markets as hedge funds or credit derivatives to some form of official regulation, or to win unfair and market-distorting tax concessions for particular interest groups – such as the reduction in Britain's standard rate of capital gains tax in 2007 following pressure from the private equity industry (which amounted to a significant incentive to ever riskier speculative investment).

Continuing denial

In the light of the historic record of economic and market performance as described above it may seem remarkable that there was so little scepticism as to the sustainability of the 1990s stock-market boom or doubts as to the wisdom of allowing it to run riot. Such doubts should only have been strengthened by the bursting of a number of emerging market bubbles – starting with that in Mexico in 1994, to be followed by similar upsets in East Asia and Russia in 1997 and 1998 – which graphically demonstrated the extent of speculative excess.

The reality of such portents – and the fact that a number of dissenting commentators and market analysts were pointing out the dangers throughout the late 1990s – suggests that the refusal of governments and market regulators to take action to put a brake on rampant markets was driven by forces other than those associated with market rationality or sound and responsible economic management. In fact it seems all too plausible to suppose that the ruling considerations were

1. the risk, amounting to virtual certainty, that any serious attempt to impose restraint – whether through greater monetary restraint or tighter regulation of financial institutions – would in any event cause a serious fall in the markets through the cumulative unwinding of massive speculative positions;

2. the reluctance of the hugely powerful vested interest represented by the leaders of the financial sector to forgo the prospect of their own personal short-term gain, and their ability to override any attempts by nominally 'independent' central banks to impose order.

Wherever the precise emphasis lay as between these considerations, the one certainty is that the public interest – in promoting long-term financial and economic stability – was seen as to a large extent subordinate. It is of course true that the prevention of a collapse in financial markets or institutions has itself long been officially regarded as a public good, to the point where governments have seen fit to intervene in the market to support the value of

securities directly. Indeed this has probably been the central factor
influencing government policy in the industrialised countries ever
since it became apparent in the 1970s that the business cycle had
not been abolished. Yet as it has become progressively clearer over
the succeeding thirty years that growth rates were set to decline
over the long term – or at least until a major crash and destruction
of capital was allowed to occur – there has correspondingly been
less and less doubt not only that such a crash was inevitable but
that the longer it was delayed the more devastating it was bound
to be. Equally, as awareness of this catastrophic reality has grown
among controlling oligarchies, so has their determination to resort
to virtually any crime or distortion in order to postpone the
day of reckoning. The practical consequences of such systematic
institutionalised deception are becoming increasingly manifest as
they now desperately seek to hold back the tidal wave of financial
collapse.

The post-millennium bubble – a terminal orgy?

All the distorting tendencies of the neoliberal era, as described
above, came together in the desperate response mounted by the
authorities (orchestrated by the US Federal Reserve) to the market
meltdown precipitated by the bursting of the dotcom bubble from
2000. This took the form of an extreme relaxation of monetary
policy from late 2001[23] – such that the benchmark US Federal Funds
rate was held at 2 per cent or less for three years from late 2001
(i.e. below the prevailing rate of price increases). Combined with
increasingly lax regulation of financial and real-estate markets
this succeeded in engineering a prolonged stock market rally from
2003 – which most media commentators chose to portray as a new

---

23. This was partly justified at the time as a way of countering the potentially
negative economic impact of the 9/11 atrocity in New York.

bull market but which has now ended in a further meltdown that has sent share prices back to the level of 1997.[24] The net result was that in the United States the total of annual net new borrowing more than doubled from \$2,016 billion in 2001 to \$4,395 billion in 2007. Such unprecedented expansion of credit – which was broadly reflected in the rate of increase in financial assets throughout the industrialised world – in turn helped fuel rates of growth in global GDP (averaging 4–5 per cent in real terms) between 2003 and 2007, higher than any recorded since the 1960s.[25]

The most remarkable, indeed frightening, aspect of this almost unprecedented surge in global growth is that any serious analyst should have understood that it was not only unsustainable beyond the short term but that it was bound to be followed by a severe slump as the huge amount of excess borrowing was unwound. By the same token the fact that all the senior government officials and regulators whose duty it was to take action to prevent such a bubble inflating wilfully shirked their responsibility is a measure of how far the entire financial establishment had surrendered to forces of reckless criminality with no concern whatever for the public interest.

A humanitarian crisis

A further measure of the criminal irresponsibility of the global leadership is that they allowed such an orgy of speculative excess to destabilise the world economy in the full knowledge that it

---

24. As of June 2009, as reflected in the US benchmark Standard & Poor's 500 index.

25. Based on IMF data. It should be noted that these may be somewhat exaggerated due to distortions in GDP measurement (notably in the USA) since the mid-1990s. See Shutt, *The Trouble with Capitalism,* pp. 194–5; also *The Decline of Capitalism: Can a Self-Regulated Profits System Survive?* (London: Zed Books, 2005), pp. 104–6.

would destroy the lives of hundreds of millions of people already struggling on the margins of existence in the Third World. This damage resulted not only from the sharp disruption of world markets and vital financial flows but also from the wild fluctuations of liberalised international commodity markets. The latter caused sharp rises in the prices of basic foodstuffs and petroleum products, which inevitably had a far more severe impact on the living standards of the world's poorest, for whom they constitute a much higher proportion of their total living costs than in industrialised countries.

Such an outcome might seem singularly ironic, not to say surreal, in light of the strenuous efforts made by the global leadership to emphasise its renewed commitment in recent years to responding to heightened popular concern all over the world at the plight of the world's poorest by devoting substantially more resources to addressing the problem. Such high-profile initiatives as the Millennium Development Goals (MDGs) enunciated by the United Nations in 2001 – with the avowed goal of eradicating global poverty by 2015 – and the much-trumpeted Make Poverty History campaign launched at the G8 summit in 2005 appeared to suggest that leaders took this commitment seriously. Yet all this rhetoric has proved hollow in the event, as the shameless insistence of international corporations on maintaining liberalised markets everywhere has trumped any consideration for the plight of the poor.

In truth such hypocrisy appears less surprising given that the G8's pious words about ending poverty came after over twenty years of forcing the whole gamut of policies consistent with neo-liberalism and globalisation (collectively known as the Washington Consensus) on developing countries as a condition of receiving development aid – during which time they had demonstrated that such policies were even more damaging to developing countries than to developed ones, with billions of people plunged deeper into poverty and hopelessness. The ruinous consequences of this approach – in terms of intensifying social disintegration, increased incidence of crime (notably narcotics-related), resort to terrorism and breakdown of state authority – have seemingly not even begun to be recognised by the global establishment, who have contributed so much to creating this disaster but are ever less inclined to address it as they struggle to preserve the global status quo intact at all costs.

2

The official response:
a study in delusion

Since the late 1970s, as noted in the previous chapter, economic policy in the industrialised countries has been driven largely by a neoliberal ideology based on an ostensible belief in free markets, deregulation and a minimal role for the state. Despite this it has continued to rely at least as much as before on the public sector to provide subsidies and support for the private sector – notably by making available profitable investment opportunities through privatisation and in its role as 'lender of last resort' to the financial sector. Understandably this extensive use of state resources to provide 'corporate welfare' is something that the political and media establishment – anxious to curry favour with their big business paymasters (see Chapter 8) – has made every effort to conceal from a public which might otherwise have been far less placid in the face of demands from their rulers to accept the need for cuts in social welfare spending and greater individual self-reliance on the part of the least well off.

It is also notable that during this thirty-year period Keynesian principles of demand management – which had been widely adopted in industrialised countries after World War II – had come to be regarded with disdain in official circles. Indeed it was generally held, not without good reason, that Keynesian methods – particularly the practice of running budget deficits so as to try to maintain high growth of GDP – had been a major source of the inflationary pressures that precipitated the financial crisis and recession of 1974–75.

Given this established official bias of the neoliberal era, it is at first sight a matter for the utmost astonishment that governments have suddenly (since 2008) resorted to extreme 'Keynesian' policies with a view to trying to resuscitate the collapsed global economy. In particular, their resort to massive budgetary deficits – tearing up all previous targets for achieving fiscal balance over the medium to long term – has been a source of widespread public amazement and, in some cases, political revulsion. In truth, however, this revelation of apparent official hypocrisy should not have been too shocking to those able to look past official propaganda with a degree of objectivity. For anyone viewing the record of the Reagan administration – supposedly the supreme exponent of neoliberal orthodoxy – would be aware that it presided over a virtual doubling of US federal debt in the 1980s as a result of its drastic tax cuts, a tendency resumed under President George W. Bush from 2001. Indeed even the most superficial analysis of fiscal policy under successive US and British administrations since 1980 demonstrates that budgetary discipline and 'prudence' have been something applied strictly to the less well-off sections of the community. In short, the whole Reagan/Thatcher neoliberal agenda was riddled with double standards from the outset.

In the case of monetary policy this propensity to extreme laxity was only to become fully apparent from 2001, when the US Federal Reserve lowered its benchmark interest rate to 1 per cent and then held it below the rate of inflation for the next four years.

As already noted, this policy – reflected in a general climate of monetary relaxation throughout most of the industrialised world[1] – was instrumental in unleashing the credit and real-estate bubbles that finally burst with such devastating effect in 2007. The surprising fact that it did not also appear to result in higher inflation is attributable partly to the impact of globalisation in enabling Western consumers to buy cheap imports from low-cost producers such as China, but also to the increasing official adoption of techniques to suppress the evidence of inflation as reflected in consumer price indices (see below).

The sudden bursting of these bubbles in 2007 led governments and central banks to undertake still more extreme relaxation of monetary policy, with base interest rates being rapidly cut to just above zero – thus emulating the policy of the Bank of Japan since the late 1990s (in its chronically unsuccessful attempts to achieve a sustained revival of growth following the 'lost decade' after the stock-market collapse of 1990). Another practice adopted by Japan (since 2001) with a view to boosting the money supply, countering deflationary pressures and thereby sustaining the level of economic activity is 'quantitative easing' – or monetising the public debt by repurchasing government debt securities with newly issued currency (otherwise known as money printing). Despite the fact that these two stratagems taken together have not succeeded in lifting the Japanese economy out of its prolonged stagnation, they had by early 2009 both been embraced by the USA and Britain.

Such a dramatic *volte-face* by governments which (particularly in the case of Britain) had for many years been proclaiming their commitment to financial orthodoxy, giving priority to price

---

1. Notwithstanding the more stringent interest rate policy of the European Central Bank, which was anxious to establish its anti-inflation credentials with the financial markets as guardian of the newly established euro.

stability, could hardly have been comforting to a public anxious for reassurance in the face of the sudden onset of an unprecedented financial crisis. For, having seen their leaders caught apparently unawares by this event, they had to listen to them justify the reversal of their earlier policies by lamely insisting that 'exceptional times demand exceptional measures'. Still less reassuring were repeated statements that the British government would do 'whatever it takes'[2] to halt the slide in the economy and restore growth – clearly implying that they did not know whether the chosen policy measures would work, a fact which Governor King of the Bank of England disarmingly confessed to the House of Commons.[3]

The first priority: bailing out the banks

An equally striking feature of the official response to the crisis has been the general determination of Western governments, led by both the Bush and Obama administrations in the USA, to spend as much taxpayers' money as necessary to prevent those major banks and other financial institutions which have been rendered insolvent – by their own imprudent and often fraudulent investments in various forms of 'toxic' assets – from collapsing totally, in line with what market forces would have dictated. The official justification given for this approach is that it is an urgent public priority that the banks' balance sheets be strengthened or recapitalised so as to permit them to resume lending to businesses or individuals whose activities would otherwise be paralysed for want of continued access to credit. At the same time, however, it was made clear when the initial bank bail-out was rushed through Congress in October 2008 that the central concern of the then

2. Gordon Brown addressing the Labour Party Conference, 19 September 2008.
3. Evidence to the Treasury Select Committee, 24 March 2009.

treasury secretary Henry Paulson (formerly chief executive of pre-eminent Wall Street investment bank Goldman Sachs) was to use the first tranche, amounting to $700 billion, to buy up a significant proportion of the banks' 'troubled assets' – a euphemism for toxic waste. However, once it became clear that these securities, which had never been traded on any public exchange, might turn out to have little or no market value – against the vast sums they represented on the banks' balance sheets – it was decided to devote the funds to other purposes rather than test their value in the markets and risk exposing the grim reality of the potential losses to the tax-paying public.

Critics of the authorities' approach – such as the Nobel prize-winning economist Joseph Stiglitz[4] – argued convincingly that the public purpose would have been better served by allowing insolvent financial institutions to go bankrupt while protecting the depositors, but at the same time creating new banks (initially at least under state ownership) – unencumbered by the toxic assets that have turned so many of the existing major banks into 'zombies' and therefore better able to provide new credit to those businesses in genuine need of it. This would, moreover, have been more consistent with the state's lender-of-last-resort role.

In principle Professor Stiglitz's solution would have been both more equitable and more cost-effective from the standpoint of the public interest. However, it seemingly failed to take account of the fact that many of these same toxic assets (particularly mortgage-backed securities) were held by other institutions such as pension funds and insurance companies, so that simply leaving their valuation to the mercy of the markets, as proposed by Stiglitz, would potentially have brought down the existing financial sector in its entirety. Hence the only solution compatible with both the

---

4. Joseph Stiglitz, interviewed on CNBC's *Power Lunch*, 4 March 2009.

public interest and financial stability would have been the outright
nationalisation of all the major insolvent institutions.[5]

The reason neither the Stiglitz solution nor anything even more
drastic was allowed to happen is that the enormously powerful
vested interests of Wall Street and the City of London success-
fully lobbied to prevent it. For they recognised that the tiny
clique of the very wealthy that they represent stood to lose vast
fortunes if the markets had been allowed to take their course
free of intervention – while equally wholesale nationalisation of
insolvent banks would have posed an existential threat to their
power, or even to the capitalist profits system in its entirety.
Rather than accept such a fate, therefore, they tried to contrive
that their bad assets be largely transferred to the state, thereby
adding unimaginable sums – officially estimated at $18 trillion
world-wide[6] – to already excessive public debt.

What seems not yet to have been grasped at the time of writing are the political implications of thus gratuitously imposing
this burden on the general public, whose welfare stands thereby
to be adversely affected, probably for decades. Thus politicians
in Britain – notably among the Conservative opposition – have
suggested that wholesale cuts in pensions and other welfare benefits will need to be accepted in order to balance the budget in
some distant future. Whether such an unscrupulous attempt
to nationalise the losses of the private sector at such enormous
social cost would prove politically acceptable must surely be open
to doubt. There are indeed already signs of strong resistance to
such brazenly unjust impositions in countries where an attempt is
being made to ensure that the reckless greed of a tiny minority

---

5. As proposed by Simon Johnson, ex-chief economist of the IMF, in 'The
Quiet Coup', *The Atlantic*, May 2009.

6. United Nations, *Summary of the World Economic Situation and Prospects 2009:
Update as of mid-2009*.

of bankers and politicians will be paid for by imposing years of austerity and privation on the mass of the population who bear no responsibility for this folly. This is particularly true of small states such as Iceland and Latvia, where the resulting increase in foreign debt has been as much as 50 per cent of GDP and public anger has been so great that the position has been compared to the war reparations imposed on Germany by the Treaty of Versailles in 1919 and foreign creditors are being pressed to accept that annual repayments will be subject to the ability to pay.[7]

Reflation of the bubble: a final throw of the dice

In truth the most alarming feature of the policy response to the crisis – which, it is already clear, has resulted in the most severe global recession since World War II – is that it cannot possibly succeed in its avowed objective of rapidly restoring the global economy to a positive growth path that could be sustained beyond the very short term. For this would require individuals and enterprises to boost their levels of consumption and fixed investment – with the aid of new loans from the financial sector – even though it is obvious that the immediate cause of the crisis has been the creation of excessive credit, leading people to spend well beyond their means. At the same time businesses, many of which already have high levels of debt on their balance sheets, are being encouraged to expand output further against a background of collapsing demand. Hence there is scarcely room for doubt that a destruction of capital – in terms of both tangible and financial assets – on a scale not seen since the 1930s (if ever) is now unavoidable.

---

7. Michael Hudson, 'Iceland's Debt Repayment Limits Will Spread', *Financial Times*, 17 August 2009. The situation is also comparable to that which caused Argentina to default on its sovereign debt in 2001.

As noted in Chapter 1, the prospect of such massive destruction – or of the radical reform of the global economy that would be needed to avert it – is viewed as politically intolerable by the ruling elite. In their desperate desire to avoid either outcome the latter have already demonstrated that they will stop at nothing (including coercion akin to blackmail and outright criminal fraud) in their efforts to avoid either the reality or the perception of systemic collapse. In fact the tendency of the authorities to use the resources of the state systematically to deceive the public over the performance of the economy can be shown to date from the 1980s, when it started to become clear that the neoliberal experiment was failing to deliver its promised benefits.

Market manipulation: the imperfectly hidden hand

One element of officially sponsored fraud aimed at ensuring market stability is the orchestrated manipulation of financial markets. It is self-evident that such manipulation must be covert, bearing in mind that investors and the public at large must not be encouraged to suspect that markets are rigged, particularly given that

- the high rewards of so many financiers are typically justified on the basis of the high risks that they run rather than trading on the basis of privileged 'insider' information;
- the public might be less willing to invest their savings in securities whose price they perceived to be determined by covert illicit manipulation rather than by the functioning of 'efficient markets' based on free and fair competition.

Until about 1990 the use of public resources to help support market prices – or 'smooth' upward or downward movements – appears to have been largely confined to Far Eastern markets, where there was the occasional barely concealed official intervention to prop up prices in the equity markets of Japan and Hong Kong (most conspicuously in the latter following the 'crash' of 1987). Yet given that such actions were perceived to be rare and confined to East Asia, they apparently raised few serious concerns among either the public or the international investor community at the time. Following the short-lived 1987 stock-market crash, however, it was decided by the Reagan administration that, given the potential scale of the collateral damage that could result from a major market collapse, price movements could not necessarily be left wholly at the mercy of random market forces. This led to the creation of the President's Working Group on Financial Markets in March 1988, a body whose *raison d'être* has never been explained to the public and whose workings are almost entirely secret, but which can have no other purpose than to orchestrate and influence market movements in such a way as to limit destabilising large swings, particularly in a downward direction. Whether it is true that, as is officially claimed, the 'Plunge Protection Team' (as it is colloquially known) never actually uses federal funds to intervene directly in markets – which is supposedly illegal – it is evidently in a position to offer incentives or de facto guarantees to non-government market players who agree to buy or sell assets at its behest.

At all events it has become clear since 2008 that the US authorities have acquired the effective power to intervene in markets directly by way of purchasing almost any assets with money they can create at will. This was indicated by Chairman Ben Bernanke of the Federal Reserve Board in announcing its proposal to undertake quantitative easing (actually first implemented in March 2009). For while this was to be used initially to buy in (or 'monetise') government debt instruments or bonds and mortgages issued by the state-sponsored mortgage funding corporations Fannie Mae and Freddie Mac, it was made clear that the purchase of private-sector debt instruments would not necessarily be excluded from such quantitative easing. Since this would make it possible to influence share prices even if no government purchase of equities were involved, it would obviously clear the way to open official manipulation of the stock market.

The US government's motives for pursuing such an approach are clearly powerful. From a purely fiscal standpoint the long bull market of 1982–2000 had made rising stock prices and the associated profits of individuals and financial institutions (including capital gains) the main source of growth in tax revenues (at a time when personal and corporate tax rates had been cut, largely as a result of the Reagan administration's so-called supply-side policies). Indeed it is evident that rising capital gains tax revenues were a significant factor enabling the Clinton administration to bring the federal budget back into balance by 2000.[8] At the same time the fabulous rewards generated for the political and corporate elite by this stock-market bonanza clearly amounted to a huge incentive for those in power to try to restore the seeming alchemy of the 1990s.

In fact it is noteworthy that by late summer 2009 (six months after it was first activated in the USA) quantitative easing had achieved conspicuous success in bidding up the price of securities – such that equities' indices had rallied to some 50 per cent above the severely depressed level of March, while the yield on Treasury bonds had been held down in spite of massive new issuance necessitated by soaring government borrowing. Yet just as most market traders and analysts were eagerly claiming that this rally signalled the end of the recession, its artificiality was emphasised

---

8. It is striking that annual receipts under this heading quadrupled between 1992 and 2000 to $121 billion, in constant 1990 prices (Congressional Budget Office), only to fall by almost 50 per cent in 2001 following the dotcom collapse.

by continuing signs of catastrophic weakness in the real economy (multiple bank failures and still soaring unemployment and house repossessions).

The fraud of official statistics

Another important facet of this growing trend to greater official misinformation is the increasing resort to falsifying statistical indicators, typically by changing the basis of calculation. A major focus of such distortion is the consumer price index, which is compiled on the basis of a weighted basket of goods from which the rate of inflation is calculated. Starting in the USA in the 1990s the practice of adjusting the price of certain products – notably personal computers and other electronic consumer goods – to take account of the impact of changing technology in enhancing their apparent utility has been widely adopted. Thus the application of this 'hedonic deflator' can have the effect of reducing the price of such goods incorporated in the index, even where the actual price to the consumer may have risen – and even though consumers may have no choice but to purchase the enhanced but more expensive product because earlier models with inferior specifications are no longer available.

The importance of these little-publicised adjustments – which, it should be noted, only ever result in downward adjustments of the index – is that

1. they not only serve to falsify the data given to the public on their cost of living, but also have the effect of reducing cost-of-living adjustments to be applied to welfare benefits such as pensions, thereby depressing the incomes of claimants below what they should rightfully be in order to hold down the level of public spending;

2. even more blatantly, they have the effect of overstating the real, inflation-adjusted level of GDP and thus the rate of growth – bearing in mind that GDP is supposed to be a faithful reflection of the actual monetary value of financial transactions as opposed to a representation of some 'shadow' valuation.

Another indicator subject to such distortion is unemployment; for even though arguably its level is no longer seen as such a central focus of public policy in the industrialised countries, governments remain concerned to manage public perceptions of it – even to the point of distorting the related official statistics. The need to engage in such deception seemingly began to be felt from about the end of the 1970s, a decade in which the recorded rate of unemployment in the OECD area doubled from 3 per cent of the labour force – roughly the level then deemed to be consistent with 'full employment', which had prevailed since 1950 – to 6 per cent. Although subsequently the rate has undoubtedly risen still higher in most of the countries concerned – to 12–15 per cent in some cases – this reality has never been reflected in the official statistics. Of the numerous subterfuges used to distort the true figures perhaps the most significant is that of reclassifying the workless as disabled – a practice followed in numerous continental European countries aside from Britain and the USA (see Chapter 7) – such that if those actually fit to work among the total receiving disability benefit were correctly classified they would probably add at least 3 per cent to the unemployment rate.[9] On this basis it may be conservatively estimated – using the criteria which were applied in the 1970s – that the overall rate of unemployment in many industrialised countries would be at least double that indicated by official statistics.

---

9. See Shutt, *The Decline of Capitalism*, ch. 6.

Aside from giving a false impression of relative prosperity, these bogus statistics may be considered useful in lending support to misinformation designed to justify misguided policy initiatives. Thus despite the long-term rise in the rate of unemployment (as measured even by official indicators) it is frequently claimed that European countries in particular are facing a structural shortage of labour – such that it will be necessary to (a) increase the inflow of migrant workers from the Third World or elsewhere, and (b) encourage or compel workers to retire later (thereby also incidentally reducing the 'burden' of their pensions on the public purse).

Such practices are symptomatic of an ever more pervasive practice among Western governments of engaging in distortion of the facts so as to mislead public opinion and thereby try to neutralise opposition. It is ironic that, in adopting this approach, they are following the traditional practice of the former Soviet Union and other Communist states, for whom statistics were and are simply another form of propaganda. It is striking, moreover, to note that repeated comments by leading commentators and journalists[10] on the growing deceptiveness of these statistics is met with uniform official silence.

Still cooking the books

Just as governments have felt it necessary to manipulate and distort official statistics, so private-sector companies are under ever more intense pressure to present their own performance in the most favourable possible light to investors. The often damaging impact of 'creative accounting' – and the sometimes less than

---

10. E.g. Kurt Richebacher, 'America's Recovery Is Not What It Seems', *Financial Times*, 5 September 2003; Richard Benson, 'The Magic Mirror Economy', Prudentbear.com, 19 March 2008.

transparent role of auditors, actuaries, credit-rating agencies and market analysts – had been dramatically revealed in the aftermath of the bursting of the dotcom bubble at the turn of the century. This episode – which precipitated the two largest bankruptcies in US corporate history (Enron and WorldCom) – caused sufficient angst in political circles to elicit the enactment of the Sarbanes–Oxley Act of 2002 (see Chapter 1). This act – the only tangible legislative result in any country of the verbal witch-hunt against the massive financial wrongdoing exposed by the dotcom collapse – provided for severe penalties (including prison) for company chief executives who signed off accounts that proved to be misleading.

It was presumably the hope of the authorities that this legislation, together with the conviction of some of the more prominent fraudsters uncovered by the financial markets debacle of 2000–01, would serve to restore investors' confidence in the integrity of the financial markets. But, as shown by the endless litany of financial scandals revealed by the renewed financial crisis of 2007–09, the pressures to meet impossible profit targets in a still largely deregulated market were such as to overwhelm any restraints against serial dishonesty. Indeed, as revealed by the Madoff and other pyramid investment frauds, there is clear prima facie evidence of criminal negligence, amounting to complicity in these crimes, on the part of federal regulators such as the Securities and Exchange Commission.

A still clearer example of the US government's determination to 'do whatever it takes' to prop up key financial institutions was the announcement in April 2009 by the Federal Accounting Standards Board (under strong pressure from the powerful banking lobby and members of Congress) that, in the case of financial companies, it would relax the established requirement under principles of fair value accounting that assets should be 'marked to market' on balance sheets, effectively allowing such companies to choose their own valuation of loans or securities where their market value was difficult to determine. Since the assets thus affected included the 'toxic waste' of asset-backed securities and collateralised debt obligations (much of it based on sub-prime mortgages) which had been the main source of the collapse that started in 2007, this move could only be seen as a desperate measure to allow the banks to use fantasy accounting to inflate the value of these assets on their balance sheets so as to boost their share prices.

However long this combination of regulatory laxity and wilful accounting distortion can manage to postpone the day of reckoning, it clearly holds enormous risks for the long-term credibility of the markets. For in the United States in particular the public's faith in the fundamental integrity of markets – that they are something more than corrupt casinos – must be seen by supporters of the system as fundamental to the long-run survival of capitalism. On the other hand it may also be the case that, as has happened in Japan since 1990, a prolonged depression in stock markets – lasting perhaps fifteen years or more – could result in the long-term or even permanent discrediting of risk-based investment in the eyes of most of the public. Equally, the same consequence could be expected in even more acute form in the event of a more dramatic collapse of asset values such as would be bound to occur if there were no official intervention to prop up the markets.

It must obviously be the fear of the global establishment that any of these possible outcomes could be terminally damaging to the survival prospects of the financial services industry on anything like its present scale – or perhaps indeed of the entire profits system itself. This is because of the important place that saving for investment has come to occupy in determining people's retirement income, thereby drawing the majority of the population, at least in the industrialised world, into a greater or lesser degree of dependence on the system's continuing to perform adequately. By the same token the flows of institutional money from pension and other funds (most of it encouraged by tax breaks) into the markets has become vital both to supporting stock prices and providing a livelihood for the millions employed in the fund-management industry. But, as evidence mounts that this can no longer be – if it ever was – a cost-effective method of providing people with an adequate retirement income (particularly in view of the huge cost to the public purse in tax breaks), it seems bound to be a gradually (or even perhaps quite rapidly) declining source of funds supporting the markets.

Going for broke

Such considerations would appear to explain the decision by the USA (under both George W. Bush and Obama administrations) – and to a greater or lesser extent all other governments of the industrialised world – to embrace without any apparent hesitation a response to the financial crisis that is at once so ideologically perverse and so manifestly unworkable. For it can scarcely be denied that the combination of extreme monetary laxity, rapid fiscal expansion and massive state subsidy of banks and other private-sector businesses constitutes a total negation of the principles of orthodox financial management as traditionally espoused by capitalist market economies. At the same time the pretence that such an unorthodox strategy could be effective in reviving growth in a situation where overborrowing by consumers had already brought the global economy to its knees bespeaks an even more total detachment from reality.

Such flagrant abandonment of both principle and realism can only be interpreted as a sure sign of total desperation on the part of the leadership. For while they must know that equilibrium can only be restored by cutting back credit and personal expenditure, rather than expanding it further, they are only too well aware that such adherence to orthodoxy in face of a hugely overblown credit bubble would spell catastrophe for the world financial system. To the extent that it is possible to discern any rationality at all in this stance it can only be based on a wild hope that further borrowing or money printing will eventually induce such a high level of inflation as to devalue outstanding debts, thereby effectively liquidating them. Yet such a policy – reminiscent of that pursued by the German Weimar Republic in 1922–23 in order to deal with its war-reparations debt under the terms of the Versailles Treaty – would clearly be fraught with enormous danger, if only because it would involve penalising the poorest and most vulnerable social groups – that is, those dependent on small, relatively fixed incomes and cash savings.

Silence of the dissidents

This intellectual bankruptcy of the leadership of the industrialised world is mirrored in the total disarray of the ideological mainstream and the inability or unwillingness of any individual or group to formulate any really distinctive approach to dealing with the crisis. Even the few who have stood out against the official commitment to underwrite the most toxic and fraudulent of banking bad debts[11] seem unwilling to confront the issue of how to cope with the now inevitable global slump, with all its ruinous consequences – beyond stressing the need for stronger regulation of finance and capital flows.

Hence the world is now embarked on a supposed recovery strategy that is both self-contradictory and doomed to failure.

---

11. Such as Professor Joseph Stiglitz – see p. 35.

Since the establishment is thus being brought face-to-face with its own ideological implosion, space may at last have been created for more open examination of the flaws of the economic system that has dominated the world for two hundred years, but has now become as hopelessly outmoded as it has always been ruinously unstable.

3

Facing up to systemic failure

It has already been observed that the central feature of the policy pursued by the leading economic powers in the years since the post-war boom came to an end around 1974 has been the increasingly frantic effort to sustain or increase the rate of growth, as measured by GDP figures. Likewise concern at the failure to fulfil this politically compelling need – reflected in the chronic decline of real growth rates in the intervening decades – lies behind both the official tendency to play down the reality of declining performance (through the distortion of statistics, inter alia) and the recklessly profligate efforts to boost economic activity since the dotcom market crash.

This characteristic desperation of the global leadership has been graphically demonstrated by their perverse insistence that the crucial action needed in response to the deep recession caused by the collapse of the overblown credit bubble since 2007 is the extension of yet more credit – notwithstanding the fact that most people (and many enterprises) are already overborrowed and in need of running down their debts. Thus once again the world has been brought up against the reality that its economic system is fatally dependent on the need endlessly to expand production of goods and services at the fastest possible rate without regard to the ability of the market to absorb them – a fundamental flaw in the model which its leaders steadfastly refuse to confront.

In fact, it is not hard to understand why the global establishment would be reluctant either to recognise or to discuss the extent of the system's dependence on sustained growth. For to do so would tend to focus attention on the fact that such dependence is part of the inescapable logic of capitalism, in that without more-or-less perpetual growth providing ever-expanding outlets for reinvestment of the profits ineluctably generated by the system it would soon wither and die. Rather, when defenders of the status quo are forced to justify their insistence on the desirability of maximising growth they fall back on the argument that it is the only way to ensure rising living standards for the poor, on the basis that 'a rising tide lifts all boats', with the most deprived benefiting from 'trickle-down' effects.

In the circumstances of the ongoing post-2007 crisis, however, the necessity from a capitalist perspective of trying to revive the level of consumption and investment (total final expenditure) has never been more stark. For without such a revival there would be no possibility of overcoming the shortfall in demand relative to productive capacity (of both capital and labour) needed to increase the rate of capacity utilisation. Superficially, it is plausible to argue that, as has happened after earlier economic slumps, sufficient balance will eventually be restored to the global economy to permit growth to be revived and a new cycle to begin. However, it needs to be pointed out that (a) there is no knowing how great the destruction of capital and livelihoods might be if the markets were allowed to take their course in this way and (b) the last comparable experience of such a steep collapse in markets and output (the 1930s) suggests that the depression may last at least a decade and require a cataclysm such as world war to bring it to an end. Moreover, even if such a prospect – with its dire social implications – could be seen as politically tolerable, there are still important reasons for doubting whether any eventual upswing in the business cycle will endure long enough to appease the huge scale of discontent that is likely to build during the prolonged decline in living standards that now appears inevitable.

Poor prospects for long-term recovery

The reasons for doubting whether in any event such a revival would be possible on a sustainable basis (i.e. for more than relatively short periods) are several.

The continuing decline in demand for capital investment

As noted in Chapter 1, this long-term trend is primarily the result of (a) a shift in the pattern of consumer demand away from manufactures towards services (which tend to be less capital-intensive) and (b) technological change (so that less capital and labour are now needed per unit of output).[1] In consequence a structural surplus of both these factors of production is likely to blight the capitalist model permanently. If that is so it would seem likely that future business cycles will be increasingly brief, with upswings being marked by more rapid lapses into largely speculative investment and consequently greater market volatility, such that over time there would be a growing perception of the chronic riskiness of asset values.

A related problem of increasing significance is the threat that advances in technology could undermine the market-based

---

1. P. Glotz, *Manifest für eine neue europäische Linke* (Berlin: Siedler Verlag, 1985), cited in A. Gorz, *Critique of Economic Reason* (London: Verso, 1989).

business models of many traditional sectors of the economy by rendering it increasingly difficult for corporate players to achieve rates of return on capital sufficient to justify their remaining in business. The most obvious instance of this phenomenon is that of cyber-technology, operating via the Internet. This has made it possible for many media and communications services to be delivered at negligible cost – in such a way as to prevent the owners of corporate assets from charging users adequately remunerative prices for their products or services. This tendency is being manifested in

- largely free access to online newspapers, thus enabling users to avoid the cost of buying the print edition (while advertising revenues are increasingly insufficient to compensate for the lost sales – all the more so as virtually free classified advertising is now being offered by such websites as Craigslist);
- for the same reasons a comparable diminution of revenues affecting purveyors of recorded music and motion pictures (and potentially printed books), as well as telephone services;[2]
- declining viability of postal services as a result of increasing resort to much quicker and cheaper email communication, ironically at the very moment when, particularly in Europe, postal services – hitherto state-owned monopolies – are being privatised in order (it is claimed) to subject them to competitive market discipline.

On top of these technology-driven threats there has arisen at the same time an apparent hostility to the very idea that profit-maximising companies should be able to capitalise on 'intellectual property' on terms which are often perceived to be unfair to users, if not also to creative artists who provide much of the content.

---

2. See Shutt, *The Decline of Capitalism*, pp. 42–3.

Perhaps the best example of this has been the emergence of providers of open-source software as the basis of computer operating systems, of which the best known is Linux. This non-proprietary software has been developed and made freely available largely as a reaction to the prolonged market dominance of Microsoft, which was for many years able to operate a de facto global monopoly; moreover, thanks to the indulgence of the US anti-trust authorities, it was allowed to apply predatory practices in order to maintain this monopoly and thereby assure exorbitant profits for itself – yet providing what many users considered to be a substandard product.

The reason such attitudes may now pose more of a threat to traditional capitalist business models than in the past would seem to be precisely the fact that it is increasingly possible to establish globally competitive enterprises with very little investment capital, especially where one can make use of the essentially free infrastructure of the Internet. Combined with the growing cultural resistance to the very idea of intellectual property rights, which in any case it may be difficult to enforce internationally, it would leave many global businesses exposed to uncontrollable competitive forces. This trend could encompass not only the electronics, telecommunications and media sectors but others where technical know-how and individual talent and expertise may be more important than access to large amounts of capital for fixed investment, such as biotechnology or even pharmaceuticals. Hence existing major enterprises in such industries – with large volumes of accumulated shareholders' funds (or 'dead capital') on which they are forced to try to make a return – could quite quickly find their very survival threatened.

The response of the 'incumbent' mega-corporations to this threat suggests that they may be powerless to avert it. Thus they have typically sought to neutralise competition from innovative start-ups by merging with them, generally at what appear or turn out to be vastly excessive valuations. Conspicuous examples have been TimeWarner's merger with AOL in 2001 and News Corporation's acquisition of MySpace in 2005. The resulting destruction of shareholder value obviously only weakens the corporations concerned without offering them much protection from similar start-up threats in future. Likewise the tendency of other corporate giants to try to sustain their profitability through mergers and acquisitions has in recent years come to be seen as increasingly questionable.[3] Thus General Electric, which in the 1990s was often referred to as 'America's most admired company', is now in danger of being seen as a corporate dinosaur – all the more so now that it has been claimed that its ability to sustain reported profit increases has depended on false accounting techniques similar to those employed by Enron (see above).[4]

For capital markets and the hugely rich and powerful financial services industry the implications of such an evolution of the economy could hardly be more menacing. This is because it would pose a clear danger that the confidence of investors in the long-term case for investing in either equities or fixed interest corporate securities could be undermined permanently. If this were to happen in the industrialised market countries generally it could easily mean they would follow the pattern set by Japan in the period since the collapse of its 1980s' stock-market boom, when the main Nikkei index has mostly languished at levels far below its all-time high of December 1989.[5] Such a prospect – which has been widely canvassed in recent years by leading

---

3. See Shutt, *The Decline of Capitalism*, ch. 3.
4. Floyd Norris, 'Inside G.E., a Little Bit of Enron', *New York Times*, 6 August 2009.
5. Less than 25 per cent of that peak as of May 2009.

commentators[6] – would naturally also imply a bleak future for the fund-management industry, representing a huge swathe of the financial services sector.

The end of any prospect of attaining 'full employment'

The prospects for the other main productive factor, labour, under such a scenario are just as grim. The extent of the growing global imbalance between the demand for and the supply of labour is virtually impossible to quantify – both because of inherent flaws in official statistical indicators of the size of the labour force, numbers employed and average hours worked (particularly in developing countries) and also because, as noted in Chapters 1 and 2, the authorities in the industrialised (OECD) countries have been at pains to distort them so as to obscure the unpalatable truth of growing structural unemployment. There can nevertheless be no doubt that the pace of global job creation is falling behind the growth of the workforce. The only available estimates of the size of the world labour force and the total numbers in employment – which are too obviously riddled with imprecision for them to be considered meaningful within a reasonable margin of error[7] – suggest that the proportion of the population in employment world-wide has been almost static or slightly declining since the 1990s. However, they take no account of the fact that there is evidence of a trend – in the great majority of countries, though not in the USA – away from what could be considered full-time

---

6. E.g. Samuel Brittan, 'The Long Death of the Cult of the Equity', *Financial Times*, 7 January 2005.

7. International Labour Organization (ILO), *Key Indicators of the Labour Market* (*KILM*), September 2007; *Global Employment Trends*, January 2009. It should be noted also that some developing countries may include in the total employed labour force family members who have worked as little as one hour a month, as well as the large numbers working in the informal sector (with no possibility of estimating the average number of hours worked overall). Hence the bare numbers of those defined as in employment seriously overstate the true quantity when expressed in full-time equivalent terms.

working.[8] Hence it is safe to infer that if an accurate estimate could be made of the utilisation of available manpower resources (labour time) in paid employment or self-employment it would show a steady long-term rise in excess capacity. Moreover, this surplus would be all the greater to the extent that account was taken of rising longevity – and consequent possible extension of the age used to define the upper limit of the workforce, traditionally 65 – in a still growing world population.

While the highly imperfect statistics may seem inconclusive, there is a mass of anecdotal evidence to lend strength to the view that the global demand for labour is in long-term decline – relative to the supply, if not in absolute terms – due to the effect of rapid technological change on productivity. A dramatic illustration of this trend is provided by Bajaj Auto Ltd, a major Indian manufacturer of motorcycles and auto rickshaws. This company had more than 21,000 workers in 1997, but by 1995 had tripled revenue by cutting the number of employees to 11,000 (partly by way of introducing robots to weld chassis frames). Likewise a study of labour market trends in India indicates that between 1994 and 2000 for every 1 per cent increase in GDP employment rose by only 0.16 per cent, whereas throughout much of the 1980s and early 1990s the same 1 per cent economic expansion produced 0.52 per cent job growth.[9]

Resistance to devaluation of capital and labour

The continuing progressive marginalisation of the role of both capital and labour is clearly a phenomenon of profound significance from a number of different perspectives. Most immediately,

---

8. In the traditional sense (as understood in industrialised countries) of working around 1,800 hours a year or more. See ILO, *KILM*, 2007.

9. Andy Mukherjee, 'India Badly Needs Jobs; Companies Hire Robots', www.bloomberg.com, 1 June 2006.

it compels us to recognise that the further devaluation of both these productive factors – under any regime of market-determined values – must entail continued relative stagnation of global production and consumption, given that it is likely to mean greater relative income insecurity for both investors and workers. This in turn will inevitably feed back into weak stock and bond markets – all the more so given that funded pension schemes will be shown to be less and less sustainable, leading to a steady dwindling of the inflow of funds to the markets from this source.

What also needs to be grasped is the damage inflicted on the global economy and on society by the ever more desperate attempts of the incumbent vested interests to resist this process of devaluation – particularly of capital. This effort is all too often reflected in misinformation and distortion of public policy through campaigns to justify support for investments of doubtful value. A well-known example of this tendency is the powerful lobbying by the biotechnology industry to promote the market for genetically modified (GM) crop varieties, to which companies such as Monsanto have committed substantial investment on which they are naturally anxious to reap maximum profit. In order to overcome strong resistance to their approval (mainly on environmental and health grounds) – notably in Europe – this lobby has devoted substantial propaganda to promoting the falsehood that without the adoption of GM varieties there will be enhanced danger of famine in poorer countries – even though it is well known to agricultural economists that globally available land resources are far more than sufficient to meet foreseeable global demand on the basis of existing technologies.[10] Further illustrations of such

10. Their success in co-opting the support of Britain's supposedly independent Food Standards Agency over this matter is likewise reflected in the Agency's persistent, and blatantly distorted, denigration of the benefits to consumers of organic foodstuffs – also in line with the interests of the same agrochemical lobby.

perniciously distorting effects of the profit motive in action are given in the next chapter.

The same vested interests are naturally far more ambivalent over the devaluation of labour, since they reflect the concerns of organised capital, which tends to favour the lowering of labour costs. However, this does not apply to the upper end of the labour market, where most members of the dominant bourgeoisie seek employment (in corporate senior management, the financial sector and professions such as law and accountancy, including consultancy). Here structures have been put in place that enable top company executives effectively to determine their own salaries (claiming nonetheless that they are in fact determined by the market in scarce executive talent), while lawyers and accountants and other consultants have been enabled to get lucrative contracts with both private- and public-sector clients on typically generous terms whose basis is similarly opaque. Meanwhile fund managers have enjoyed a comfortable existence based on the massive tax subsidy to pension schemes which are inherently unviable and have for years only been able to record a surplus based on more or less false accounting.

At the bottom of the scale, in contrast, the vast mass of employees without scarce specialist skills have seen a steady decline in their levels of pay in relative terms, notably in the USA (see Chapter 1). At the same time the loss of bargaining power of organised labour is further reflected in the fact that it has been unable to prevent the imposition of longer working hours in industrialised countries; thus whereas European trade unions had made considerable progress by 1990 in establishing a basic 35-hour week for full-time workers (notably in France), by the first decade of the new century they were struggling to prevent it being increased back to 40 hours or more.

The need to abandon the growth obsession

Once the inescapable reality of the bleak outlook for investment and the financial markets is accepted it must inevitably follow that the pursuit of indiscriminate growth maximisation is not only futile but damaging to the prospects of attaining other more vital economic and social objectives, such as the reduction (if not elimination) of poverty. This is because, as the history of the thirty-year neoliberal era now ending abundantly illustrates, ever more desperate efforts to sustain the return on capital (against a background of diminishing need for it) – and in the process to keep lifting the value of the related securities – inevitably tend to result in progressively greater economic distortion and misallocation of resources. What is most striking about this syndrome – at a time when there has ostensibly been a widespread commitment to a laissez-faire ideology and 'rolling back the frontiers of the state' – is that government intervention and de facto subsidies have become increasingly crucial to incentivising and protecting investments, with a view to sustaining the rate of return on them and thereby facilitating continued growth. Therefore, if for no other reason than to avoid the further negative consequences of such intervention – which are described at length in the next chapter – governments will need explicitly to renounce the maximisation of GDP growth as an economic policy concern in favour of prioritising more specific objectives to be met in line with both democratic choices and the available resources.

If this were not a sufficient reason for dethroning the god of growth, another equally compelling one has begun to loom increasingly large at the start of the twenty-first century. This is what may be defined under the general heading of the environmental constraint to perpetually expanding output. The aspect of this phenomenon which has become the greatest focus of public concern is that of global warming, associated with rising carbon emissions resulting from the inexorable growth in production of energy based on fossil fuels. The precise extent of the threat that this poses and the appropriate way to deal with it are matters of considerable controversy, and it is by no means clear exactly what impact the response will have on the pattern of economic development in the medium to long term. Thus it may prove quite feasible, as some experts have suggested,[11] to develop a renewable energy source – such as solar power – to the point where it can be substituted for most fossil-based energy at negligible cost, thereby effectively removing this constraint to growth. Yet if this is indeed the case it is ironic that the biggest obstacle to realising such a beneficial technological breakthrough might turn out to be the vested interest of the major oil companies and other energy giants, which, in seeking to protect their existing investments in the sector, have become some of the most vociferous lobbyists against what they claim to be the 'scare story' of man-made global warming (see also Chapter 4).

However, even if the problem of global warming could be neutralised as an obstacle to continued economic growth, other environmental constraints to expansion of production would remain to be addressed – and may well prove more intractable. These relate to physical limitations imposed by a finite planet which is ever more overpopulated (see below) – particularly in relation to vital scarce resources such as land (as witness resistance to airport expansion in Britain and continuing concerns over ever-growing traffic congestion on the roads), fresh water supply and marine fisheries. In fact it is a disturbing reflection on how far the pernicious influence of the profit motive may have distorted the public discourse on environmental concerns that the issue

11. E.g. Ray Kurzweil, cited in Ed Pilkington, 'The Future is Going to be Very Exciting', *Guardian*, 2 May 2009.

of global warming has come to be such a dominant concern at the expense of others which are (a) more amenable than global warming to effective remedial action at national rather than international level, and (b) just as potentially harmful to human welfare (e.g. air and water pollution).[12] The impact of the vested interests involved in determining policy in this area is described further in Chapter 4.

A related phenomenon – the apparently growing resistance to consumerism, at least among certain sections of the public – could well be tending to undermine corporate sales and profits even further. One particularly influential factor behind this, aside from rising concerns about the environment, is greater health consciousness. This is especially significant in the relatively wealthy OECD countries, where such phenomena as obesity – reflected in higher incidence of heart disease and diabetes – are increasingly rife, as are alcoholism and smoking-related diseases. At the same time these concerns of individuals are mirrored in growing official preoccupation with the potential harm to public health (and the related harm to the economy from the higher cost of treatment) resulting from excess consumption of harmful substances. By the same token it is becoming more widely recognised that, under the profits system, the desire of consumers to contain or reduce their consumption of these substances and improve their diet – and the concern of the authorities to support them in this – are in conflict with the corporate compulsion to pursue the maximisation of profit and thus consumption of their products.

A more stark, if less publicised, demonstration of the pernicious impact of commercially driven consumerism – and the limits to it – is provided by the growth in dissemination of pornography and its increasingly hardcore nature. The rise of this global market has

12. See 'The Great Climate Change Hijack', BBC Radio 4, 27 August 2009.

been facilitated by the relaxation of legal restrictions in the USA since the 1970s – and latterly by the spread of the Internet. What is striking is that a development which was originally justified as an acceptable response to the demands of libertarians in the permissive era of the 1960s and 1970s has been driven by competitive pressures to purvey progressively more extreme hardcore images – to the point where even some of the original advocates of liberalisation (including well-known pornographer Larry Flynt) have expressed their disgust. At the same time there is significant evidence that the increasing availability of such material among traditional communities in Africa and other developing regions is having a socially disastrous impact – leading to a marked rise in the incidence of rape and HIV – while participants in the production of hardcore porn movies (mainly in California) find their physical and mental health is threatened in an industry which treats them as akin to prostitutes.[13]

Excess population growth – the undeclared menace

Of all the major threats to the future sustainability of human civilisation the least discussed is that of overpopulation. This is all the more remarkable given that the world's population has grown at unprecedented speed since the end of World War II, having nearly tripled in that period to almost 7 billion – such that it might have been supposed that the capacity of the planet's finite land mass to sustain such rapid growth would be a matter of greater concern. Moreover, once it became clear, as it has been at least since the 1980s, that technological advance was tending to create a structural labour surplus on a global scale, it should logically have been queried as to whether the implied need to expand productive

13. See 'Hardcore Profits', BBC 2, 30 August and 6 September 2009.

capacity proportionately even faster than population growth would be physically sustainable – even assuming the market could absorb the extra output.

Yet so far from addressing this problem the global establishment has in the main strenuously sought to ignore it or pretend it does not exist. Thus while developing countries are the ones most severely affected by rising population – having the highest growth rates and being most seriously exposed to the environmental consequences because of the relatively heavy concentration of people in rural areas – support for family planning in aid programmes has been almost totally lacking. Indeed it has been actively opposed, with the strong support of the Roman Catholic Church and other religious organisations, by donor agencies and governments (most conspicuously that of the USA under George W. Bush). Hence the striking fact that two of the MDGs are the achievement of universal primary education and reduction of child mortality by two-thirds, which are arguably conflicting objectives in the absence of any reference to reducing population growth rates.

Astonishingly, in fact, it appears still to be the official view in many countries – although not in China and India – that high population growth is actually a desirable development, even though it is demonstrable that the most prosperous countries are those with relatively low population growth rates. Although the official justification for this apparently perverse position is pseudo-religious, there seems little doubt that it is more rooted in the perception of the ruling establishment that rising population on a global scale is beneficial to the attainment of high GDP growth rates – perhaps on the assumption that billions of new consumers will take up the slack created by fading appetites in the industrialised world – and that it also helps to maintain an abundance of labour, thereby tending to depress its cost.

In face of the inexorable long-term trends described in this chapter one might suppose that world leaders will be forced to recognise that – coming on top of the present cyclical economic collapse – there is not only no chance of reviving growth for the immediate future but very little prospect of ever returning to the relatively high growth rates of the past on a sustained basis. Once this nettle is grasped the necessity to seek a new economic model compatible with negligible growth for the indefinite future will also become self-evident. In that event it would also become possible to eliminate the grotesque distortions and perversions produced by the increasingly futile attempt to prevent the existing model from collapsing, as illustrated in the next chapter.

4

The price of profit-driven growth

As noted in the previous chapter, in the struggle to sustain the rate of profit and thereby try to avoid the 'bust' phase of the business cycle substantial distortions have been introduced into the functioning of the economy, generally with the active or passive assistance of governments. While many of these changes have been highly beneficial to corporate profitability, in most cases they are extremely costly in terms of public welfare. The latter has also been adversely affected by the diversion of scarce state resources to the often counterproductive pursuit of economic growth, whose sole beneficiary is increasingly shown to be the profit-maximising corporate sector. This chapter seeks to illustrate this tendency by examining some of the more obvious ways in which this policy orientation is damaging to the public interest.

The privatisation catastrophe

A conspicuous innovation of the neoliberal era has been the extensive resort to the privatisation of state-owned enterprises and assets in virtually all countries. Its widespread adoption is attributable to the fact that it was foisted on virtually all developing countries as one of the conditions – in line with the Washington Consensus – of their receiving aid from the International Monetary Fund or the World Bank. A remarkable facet of this tendency was that belief in it so rapidly became the conventional wisdom – on the grounds that private ownership of enterprises was claimed to be self-evidently more cost-effective than public ownership – even though the state ownership of utilities such as water supply and telecommunications had been the largely unchallenged norm throughout the world since the nineteenth century (not least because most such services were generally considered to be natural monopolies where competition was either impossible or inappropriate). Just as extraordinary is the fact that virtually none of either the critics or champions of privatisation has ever sought to address the obvious suspicion that its real purpose was to provide investment outlets for otherwise redundant private capital.[1]

Whatever the theoretical merits or demerits of privatisation, it is by now widely perceived (even in Britain, where the Thatcher government may be said to have pioneered the idea in the 1980s) that in practice it has almost always worked to the ultimate detriment of consumers, workers and taxpayers, demonstrating the malign impact of applying the private profit motive to vital public services. Thus, for example,

1. Public assets have frequently been transferred to private investors at values far below their true market worth – notably in the case of the sale of British Rail's rolling stock in 1996 and the sale of a substantial share of the equity of Qinetiq (previously the British government's Defence Evaluation and Research Agency)

---

1. As pointed out in Shutt, *The Trouble with Capitalism*, in 1998.

in 2003 to privileged insiders at a price which was only about
10 per cent of what it was found to be worth on its subsequent
flotation in 2006. Taxpayers were thus robbed of hundreds of
millions of pounds.

2. The terms on which the public regulators in Britain assess the
   pricing regimes and investment strategies of privatised utilities
   (particularly ones where meaningful competition cannot be
   assured, such as water supply) are such as to encourage overinvestment in fixed capital, given that the allowable return
   on capital (and thus charges to users) is set on the basis of a
   hypothetical market rate which effectively guarantees a stream
   of profit on whatever investment is allowed. The inevitable
   result is that consumers have to pay more than they would
   under a non-profit regime where there was no bias in favour
   of maximising capital investment – not to mention the loss to
   the economy from the inefficient utilisation of resources.

3. Ineffectiveness of regulation. As has long been known – notably
   from the experience of the United States, where private ownership of public utilities and services has long been the rule rather
   than the exception – statutory regulators, whose function is to
   protect the public interest by ensuring that the quality and
   price of services to consumers is reasonable, tend to be subject
   to 'capture' by the firms they are supposed to be regulating.
   In other words they are liable to be lobbied, pressurised or
   otherwise seduced into allowing providers to cut corners or
   raise prices. By definition there is no way of insuring against
   this happening or of estimating its incidence. However, there
   seems little doubt that it is extremely commonplace – if only
   from anecdotal evidence – and thus adds significantly to costs
   borne by users. This point is tellingly illustrated by a recent
   example from Britain, where in 2008 the Severn Trent Water
   company was convicted of deliberately falsifying leakage data

presented to the regulator (Ofwat) in order to justify a price increase. The significance of this incident is that it only came to light because it was revealed by a conscientious 'whistleblower' from inside the company. Hence it is hard not to suppose that many more such incidents occur without the regulator finding out or challenging such data.[2]

4. Although privatisation deals – including partnership arrangements under the British private finance initiative (PFI) – have been justified on the basis that they strengthen public finances by allowing any risks arising from cost overruns on investment or failure to meet performance targets to be fully transferred to the private-sector operators, this has proved a totally hollow commitment in practice. This is because it is well known to all concerned that vital public services – such as the troubled British rail franchises and the British Airports Authority (see also below) – could not be allowed to fail financially and cease trading. Indeed the currently unfolding post-2007 crisis has brought to light the commitment of the government to indemnify the private rail operators against most of their potential losses due to a downturn in revenues caused by falling traffic.[3] Similarly in the US healthcare sector (which has always been and remains dominated by private for-profit companies) the healthy returns on capital have become largely dependent on the funds provided by the federal government's Medicare and Medicaid programmes aimed at the elderly and low-income groups.

2. Moreover the likelihood that such practices will be repeated is arguably all the greater in that, although this was a criminal conviction for fraud, the fines imposed on the company amounted to only about 12 per cent of one year's profits and it was decided that none of the responsible executives would be prosecuted (with some even going on to other senior positions in the water industry) or, apparently, sued by the company – see 'Disgraced Severn Bosses Still Earn a Mint', *Financial Mail*, 13 April 2008, thisismoney.co.uk.

3. 'Payouts to Rail Operators Set to Soar', *Observer*, 24 May 2009.

It is highly illustrative of the degenerate state of the body politic in what are claimed to be the world's most developed countries that the manifold failures and crimes which have occurred as a result of the privatisation process have received so little publicity. Thus most of the information cited above in relation to Britain has only come to light as a result of investigations by fringe papers such as the satirical magazine *Private Eye* and a tiny number of dedicated journalists working for more mainstream newspapers.[4] The fact that the abysmal record of the whole project has not been a subject of more in-depth analysis in the media or at the political level speaks volumes for the corrupting power of big business in subverting the interests of the public so as to protect its own.

Forcing enterprises to service surplus capital

As well described by Karl Marx, one of the most pernicious features of capitalism is the necessity it imposes on the private business sector of finding ways to generate sufficient returns on the ever-expanding stock of accumulated 'surplus value'. Naturally the difficulty of doing this becomes more acute the longer the upswing of a business cycle continues without a market collapse being allowed to destroy capital value on a significant scale. As this problem has intensified during the neoliberal era – from the mid-1970s (see Chapter 1) – financiers and investors have shown prodigious ingenuity in devising new ways of overcoming it, though inevitably always at the expense of the other claimants on value-added – whether workers, welfare dependants, other consumers or even existing shareholders (including funds representing the livelihoods of actual and future pensioners).

---

4. George Monbiot, 'The Real British Expenses Scandal Seems to Be Immune to Exposure', *Guardian*, 25 May 2009.

A particularly damaging practice has been that of loading corporate balance sheets with extra debt so as to impose an additional claim on value-added. This has typically been achieved by means of a takeover or 'buy-out' of a company – whether by the corporate raiders of the 1980s (as portrayed in Oliver Stone's 1987 movie *Wall Street*) or the private equity buyers of the 2000s (see Chapter 1) – which is then restructured away from the glare of the public markets with a view to selling it off at a profit, but invariably with a much larger burden of debt on its balance sheet. While such manoeuvres are always justified by claims that they are a means of improving the efficiency and profitability of the business by introducing more dynamic management, the more brutal reality is that the companies concerned typically end up more financially vulnerable because of the higher level of debt imposed on them. All too often, in order to service this debt and thus swell the returns to otherwise redundant capital, workers and customers – not to mention taxpayers – are squeezed and the long-term future of the business jeopardised, while the speculative investors typically sell out their interest at a large profit at the earliest opportunity.

The consequences of this may be especially negative where the company concerned operates a key public service, as was revealed by the takeover of the privatised British Airports Authority (BAA) by Ferrovial of Spain in 2006 for £10.3 billion – but with the aid of £17.5 billion of additional debt on the balance sheet of the parent company. In order to service this debt the company – which operates a monopoly at London's three main airports[5] – was forced to raise user charges by over 20 per cent in one year, 2008–09 (with the acquiescence of the regulator, the Civil Aviation Authority). This increase consequently had to be reflected in higher passenger

---

5. It controls Heathrow, Gatwick and Stansted airports.

fares, although – as the airlines understandably complained – the increase was not justified on the basis of improvements in the facilities and appeared rather to be a breaking of the regulator's commitment at the time of the takeover that BAA would not be allowed to raise charges to pay for its increased debt. A potentially similar instance of the malign impact of 'leveraged' buyouts of privatised corporations in Britain concerns several water and power utilities, which in the process were allowed by the regulators to take on high levels of debt before the credit crunch of 2007, which independent observers have suggested they may consequently have difficulty in servicing, thus jeopardising their ability to carry out essential maintenance of the infrastructure – and ultimately posing the risk of interruption to these vital public services.[6]

Many other examples of this tendency could be cited, such as the effects of buyouts of major British pub chains since 2000, where the resulting additional loading of debt onto their balance sheets is estimated to have resulted in an extra 50 per cent on the price of a pint of beer.[7] Such are the true costs to the economy of allowing the parasite of excess capital to swell and run rampant across different sectors.

The private pensions vampire

Perhaps the single most wasteful and ruinous misallocation of resources imposed on society by the contemporary profits system has been the funded pensions industry. Private funded pension schemes, which were first introduced on any scale in the United States in the 1950s and have since spread to Britain and other

6. Richard Wachman, 'Utilities At Risk from Debt Timebomb', *Observer*, 20 April 2008.
7. Fair Pint Campaign, 'Calling Time on the Tie', 20 May 2009, www.fairpint. org.uk; 'Tied and Emotional', *Private Eye*, 11 June 2009.

(mainly Anglo-Saxon) countries, are supposed to build up funds – via contributions from employers and employees – that are invested so as to yield sufficient income to pay a defined level of pension benefit to scheme members (usually related to their final salary) on reaching retirement age. In practice this has proved to be a far more expensive and less reliable method of providing pensions than state 'pay-as-you-go' schemes (which are not invested and pay pensions out of current income), in that

- their running costs are far higher than the non-funded state schemes;
- they have proved unable to meet their liabilities over the long term – once they (a) reach maturity and find themselves with more retired members receiving benefit than ones still working and paying contributions, and (b) have to withstand a prolonged decline in global equity markets such as the one that began in 2000;
- their cumulative deficits[8] constitute an ever more onerous burden for the sponsoring companies – such that, for example, they were a major contributing factor in the bankruptcy of General Motors in 2009;
- in the last resort they have had to be bailed out by governments at huge cost to the taxpayer – on top of the cost of the tax breaks allowed to them on contributions.

Despite this disastrous reality the political and media establishment in Britain and elsewhere continues to be co-opted in a campaign of barefaced, endlessly repeated lies, mainly designed to discredit the far more efficient and successful public pay-as-you-go system, to the effect that

---

8. These have often been understated (or their surpluses overstated) as a result of actuaries fraudulently using bogus assumptions on life expectancy or asset valuations.

1. such public-sector schemes (including the occupational schemes of civil servants, teachers and others) are becoming unaffordable because of their 'unfunded liabilities' – even though, being pay-as-you-go rather than funded schemes, by definition they cannot have unfunded liabilities;

2. increasing longevity means that the rising 'dependency ratio' (of retired workers receiving pensions to those still working and paying contributions) will soon result in the capacity of the latter to support the former being stretched to breaking point – even though there is no evidence to suggest that this trend (which has been in progress for decades) has put the financing of these schemes under strain; in fact, thanks to rising productivity in the economy generally, there is no reason whatsoever why it cannot continue to do so – so that the dependency ratio is shown to be a meaningless concept.

What is scarcely appreciated by the general public is that the continuing political support for the totally perverse system of private funded pensions – and the desperate campaign of misinformation designed to ensure its retention – is entirely a function of corrupt lobbying by the sole ultimate beneficiaries, the fund management firms in the City and Wall Street.

Wasteful and costly over-investment

We have already observed how the ever more desperate search for outlets for the surplus accumulated capital generated by the profits system has led to wasteful and often destructive investment in privatised industries and other businesses subject to speculative buyout. This tendency also extends to other sectors, especially where the public sector is involved or can be readily co-opted to subsidise or protect private profit-seeking investment.

A conspicuous example of such a costly and almost certainly non-viable investment which has nevertheless become a focus of much private-sector interest in Britain and elsewhere is nuclear power. In order to meet the undoubted need for new power generation capacity in Britain by 2020 the government has decided to put most emphasis on the development of nuclear power, with strong support from a powerful lobby representing the power-generation industry and other private-sector interests. There are apparent advantages of nuclear power in respect of its low carbon-intensity – a vital consideration in relation to achieving national targets for reduction of the industry's contribution to global warming. However, given its undeniably high overall production costs and thus doubtful cost-competitiveness, it is on the face of it surprising that both industry and the government should prefer this option. This point is underlined by the fact that the government only succeeded in privatising the existing nuclear power plants in 1996 (several years after the rest of the industry) by indemnifying the private investors in the company (British Energy) against the potentially massive decommissioning costs of the existing reactors, while even without this burden the company had difficulty in competing and had to be bailed out – and effectively renationalised – in 2004.

In view of these serious constraints, not to mention fierce opposition from environmentalist pressure groups, it may be inferred that there is a hidden agenda in the industry's determined effort to secure commitment to a major expansion of nuclear power. Based on our earlier analysis it seems equally self-evident that this agenda is centred on two related considerations:

1. The huge capital-intensiveness of nuclear power production, such that capital costs typically amount to as much 70 per cent of total costs; the attractions of this prospect for investment institutions looking for outlets for surplus capital are obvious.

2. The plausible supposition (based on past experience) that the government can be induced to underwrite not only the decommissioning costs but any other cost overruns, such that an acceptable return on capital for private investors will be assured regardless of the true economic cost. (It should be noted that similar considerations appear to lie behind the interest of investors – with strong political support, notably in Britain, the USA, Denmark and Germany[9] – in the development of wind-power generation, in preference to other forms of renewable energy, since capital costs are also relatively high and government subsidies substantial; this despite widely expressed doubts as to its economic viability and environmental costs and the fact that to date it has not made possible the closure of any of the thermal power stations to which it is supposedly an alternative.)

Other examples of costly, non-viable and unnecessary projects, which seem designed primarily to absorb excess capital, abound in Britain. Thus, for example, huge computer-based data-processing projects in the National Health Service – contracted to (mainly US) information technology companies – have absorbed hundreds of millions of pounds and have been the subject of many cost overruns, delays and operational malfunctions. The fact that this does not cause more of a public outcry may be due to the fact that they are designed to meet imaginary needs such as greater 'patient choice' rather than genuine priority concerns of the tax-paying public – so that when they fail to perform they are not necessarily missed. Of the many other comparable instances that could be cited in other public services the most notorious and potentially costly of all is perhaps that linked to the Labour government's introduction of a national identity card scheme, starting in 2009. If, as is widely

---

9. In Britain the wind lobby has even managed to co-opt the environmentalist campaigning group Friends of the Earth.

asserted, the scheme fails to achieve public acceptance and would not in any event achieve the intended aim of significantly enhancing national security, the huge cost – at least £6 billion – would benefit only the private-sector contractors involved.

Another instance of the waste too often resulting from the symbiotic relationship of the state and the private corporate sector is that of state-funded urban regeneration programmes – perhaps the most popular form of economic 'pump priming' often associated with the ideas of Keynes. Ironically the vogue for these schemes began in the United States in the 1970s, just as Keynesian theories and 'corporatism' were supposedly going out of fashion. The political attractions of these schemes – whose avowed purpose has been to use public investment in major construction projects and improved infrastructure to stimulate an inflow of substantially greater amounts of private investment into run-down industrial areas, thereby creating new enterprises and jobs – has continued into the present century despite their conspicuous failure to achieve much (if any) lasting benefit. For in practice research has shown that their main effect has been to create short-term opportunities for profitable real-estate speculation, but with hardly any durable benefit to the community in terms of new jobs or improvement to the quality of those lives blighted by industrial decline.[10]

Profit-distorted priorities

Just as the pressure to find investment outlets for excess capital has led to the kind of subsidised misallocation of resources described above, so the compulsion to meet high target rates of return

---

10. See E. Swyngedouw, F. Moulaert and A. Rodriguez, 'Large Scale Urban Development Projects: A Challenge to Urban Policy in European Cities', in *Urban Redevelopment and Social Polarisation in the City* (European Union, DG XII, 1999).

on capital has deterred private-sector corporations – whether privatised or not – from undertaking investment that is genuinely needed in the public interest. This tendency – along with other anti-social practices stemming from profit-driven motivation – can be illustrated by considering developments in the economically crucial pharmaceuticals and energy sectors.

Pharmaceuticals: a classic conflict of public and private interests

This industry has an obviously vital role in advancing public health and welfare through the cost-effective application of medical science. Its success in achieving this aim is determined by research into new products, which tends to be very costly and uncertain in its outcome. The consequently high risks for profit-driven companies are offset by (a) a substantial degree of public subsidy for basic research and (b) guaranteed high prices (particularly in the USA) for a limited period under state-funded healthcare programmes. Given this degree of public commitment to supporting the industry it might be supposed there would be corresponding official determination to ensure that the private-sector companies involved operate in compliance with publicly determined priorities. In at least two respects, however, governments, particularly in the USA, have effectively conceded that the profit-maximising priorities of 'big pharma' should take precedence.

• *Priority targets for research.* There has evidently been very little attempt by the world's governments to pressurise the industry into committing resources to conquering major global scourges such as HIV, malaria and tuberculosis. Rather they seem all too willing to accept the industry's frank admission that, since these are primarily diseases of the developing world (i.e. affecting poor people with little or no money), there is insufficient profit in trying to develop drugs to combat them such as would attract the interest of profit-driven companies.[11] Instead it is seen as quite normal that they should devote huge resources to developing highly profitable treatments for 'erectile dysfunction' – a less than life-threatening malady of concern mainly to higher income groups.

- *Product approval.* New drugs developed by pharmaceuticals companies need to be approved by national regulatory authorities before they can be marketed. These bodies, of which the US Food and Drug Administration (FDA) is by far the most important (covering the world's largest single drug market), have an extremely onerous responsibility, given the need to guard against approving products that may have unduly harmful side effects relative to any gains to individuals' health which may result – thus avoiding any repeat of the Thalidomide tragedy, which affected mainly European countries around 1960. Equally they must validate – with rigorous testing procedures – the effectiveness of drugs in treating the conditions they are supposed to. At the same time, however, the regulators are under constant pressure from the manufacturers to approve new drugs so as to sustain the flows of revenue and profits in line with the demands and expectations of shareholders and stock markets. There is little doubt that this pressure has intensified since around 2003 as the number of new drugs approved has declined, for reasons partly to do with the lack of new scientific breakthroughs. This has occurred, moreover, following enactment of legislation whereby drug companies can pay fees to the FDA for testing treatments in return for a guarantee of an early decision on whether to approve them or not. In these circumstances it is scarcely surprising that allegations of 'capture' of the FDA by the drug companies have increased – amid evidence of declining

---

11. See Jean-Pierre Garnier, 'A Prescription for Combating Global Diseases', *Financial Times*, 30 May 2005.

safety and quality. Thus it has been claimed that, as of 2005, out of 538 leading medicines prescribed for use in the USA as many as 181 were unsafe or ineffective. Particular concern was aroused by the scandal surrounding the anti-inflammatory drug Vioxx marketed by Merck, which was approved in 1999 but had to be withdrawn from use in 2004 after it was found to have caused heart attacks in patients (subsequently estimated at over 130,000 in the USA alone).[12]

Energy

It has become obvious since the 1970s that assuring an appropriate supply of energy at acceptable cost and with minimum damage to the environment is a matter of ever more central public concern – in relation both to the continued functioning of the economy and even to the survival of the human species on a habitable planet. Despite this it has remained an article of faith among the global leadership that the ownership and control of the sector should remain in predominantly private hands and that it should be managed in such a way as to put profit-seeking private interests (including those of energy traders) ahead of those of the public. Of the many manifestations of this tendency that could be cited we may mention in particular:

• *Unprofitability of exploration and extraction.* For all the increasing awareness of the growing scarcity of oil and gas reserves and the vital importance to national and global economic stability of maintaining adequate global supplies, the major oil companies have felt no compulsion to make the investment in exploration and infrastructure necessary to secure new sources of supply for the future. Instead they have effectively refused to make the

---

12. Andrew Jack, 'Master or Servant: The US Drugs Regulator under Scrutiny', *Financial Times*, 7 January 2005.

relatively minor investments needed to extend the extraction potential of existing oil fields – notably in the British section of the North Sea – without the incentive of additional tax breaks, preferring instead to return their substantial profits to shareholders. As a leading sector expert has pointed out, 'there is a serious danger that short-termism driven by demands of the stock market ... may prove to be seriously damaging to oil consumers.'[13] At the same time the companies cite wildly fluctuating oil and gas prices as another deterrent to investment in both exploration and refining capacity (where periodic shortages have also helped to generate destabilising price rises for refined products). Despite such warnings one option never even mentioned in political or media discussion of the issue is the possibility that governments should assume a direct role in either influencing the investment and production strategies of the oil companies or regulating market prices, sharp fluctuations in which have proved to be particularly harmful to the economic and social welfare of poor countries. This is most obviously because to do so would tend to threaten the autonomy and the profits of the very powerful corporate vested interests involved, as well as those of the traders making huge speculative profits from the 'free' market price fluctuations which they themselves are able to manipulate to a great extent. In fact, just as it can be shown that investment generally has become ever more speculative rather than productive in the neoliberal era (see Chapter 1), a case could be made for the view that the oil majors have seen it as more profitable to engage in speculation in and manipulation of the market values of their products than in trying to meet the demand for them.

---

13. Professor Paul Stevens of Dundee University quoted in 'Tough Choices for Oil Companies in the Quest to Head Off a Global Capacity Crunch', *Financial Times*, 22 September 2004.

- *Lip-service to the green agenda.* A striking example of the anti-social consequences of maintaining the world's major oil and gas companies in purely private ownership is provided by their attitudes to the issue of global warming, now widely recognised as a matter of vital importance to the public interest for the foreseeable future. Yet ExxonMobil (the world's largest company) has made no secret of its long-standing support for groups dedicated to discrediting the idea that man-made global warming was a threat that could be mitigated by cuts in carbon emissions, even though it has recently reduced this support, admitting that it has served to 'divert attention' from the need to find new sources of clean energy.[14] In some contrast BP and Shell have both been quick to distance themselves from such reactionary forces and publicly commit themselves to including renewable energy projects in their investment strategies (to the accompaniment of hugely expensive publicity campaigns) – even to the point, in the case of BP, of rebranding itself as 'Beyond Petroleum' instead of British Petroleum and giving itself a 'solar' logo. Yet this has not prevented both companies using the post-2007 global recession – which has been marked by sharp falls in oil and gas prices – as an excuse to announce cutbacks in their investments in renewables. In justifying this a spokesman for Shell stated: 'We are businessmen, and we put the money we have available for investment into the opportunities that give us the best returns for the shareholders. If those were in renewables today, we'd be putting money there… It's just not the case.'[15] Such a clear statement of corporate logic is a salutary reminder of the ultimately irreconcilable

---

14. 'Exxon to Cut Funding to Climate Change Denial Groups', *Guardian*, 28 May 2008.

15. 'BP, Shell Renewable Invest Cuts Make Business Sense', *Wall Street Journal*, 25 March 2009.

conflict between public interest and private profit – exploding as it does the expensively cultivated myth of 'corporate social responsibility'.[16]

- *Limited interest in conservation.* Although there is overwhelming evidence that the most cost-effective approach to reducing carbon emissions is through energy conservation (e.g. improved insulation of buildings) – such that it has been estimated that it could cut non-transportation energy consumption (and corresponding carbon emissions) in the USA by 23 per cent and pay for itself twice over in ten years[17] – it has received far less investment or government support than the development of renewables, not to mention continuing public subsidy of fossil-fuel production. This attitude on the part of the private-sector energy companies is scarcely surprising since such a strategy would imply reduced production, investment and profit levels. That governments such as the British should have not merely acquiesced in this view but exacerbated the position by extending privatisation of the industry is a measure of the relative importance it gives to investor interests over the public interest.

Drawing together all the various aspects of private- and public-sector interaction relating to energy and its conservation addressed in this chapter (as well as other pressing environmental issues – see Chapter 3), it is striking how far private commercial vested interests have come to dominate the formation of official policy in this area of vital public concern – and with what hugely negative consequences for the public interest. Thus not only have these profit-maximising interests sought to discredit the idea that

---

16. See Shutt, *The Decline of Capitalism*, pp. 82 and 98.
17. *Unlocking Energy Efficiency in the US Economy*, McKinsey, August 2009, www.mckinsey.com.

global warming and other environmental constraints constitute
a serious threat to human welfare requiring a policy response;
to the extent that they are at last compelled to come to terms
with the reality of the problem they have sought to ensure that
government policy is directed

1. to support those responses – such as investing in capital-
   intensive alternative energy sources of doubtful economic
   viability but subsidised by the state – which favour maximum
   levels of private investment with guaranteed levels of profit;
2. to give least emphasis to what is evidently the most cost-
   effective type of investment for reducing global warming
   – energy conservation – since this would reduce production
   and consumption of energy, to the detriment of corporate
   profits; and
3. to marginalise those environmental problems, such as air and
   land pollution, which could be largely solved at national level,
   in favour of focusing mainly on that of climate change, which
   can only be dealt with, if at all, by international agreement
   (the net effect of which, conveniently for those seeking to
   delay curbs on emissions and related energy production, will
   be to postpone effective action for many years – see also
   Chapter 3).

Encouragement to speculation
through liberalisation of markets

The evident propensity of capitalists since the 1970s to compensate
for the lack of profitable outlets for their surplus profits in productive investment by shifting the emphasis more and more to (essentially unproductive) speculation has already been referred to. This
is in itself a damning indication of the inherent propensity of the
profits system to misallocate resources. However, it fails to reflect

the serious economic damage arising from the deployment of this speculative capital – which has in any case been multiplied many times over through bank leverage in the increasingly permissive financial climate of the last three decades. The consequent swelling of the 'wall of money' overhanging global financial markets has naturally given rise to an ever greater volume of funds being deployed in purely speculative investments, particularly in the huge and highly liquid global markets for currencies and commodities, where by now trillions of dollars are invested every day in both hedging positions (i.e. to ensure against price rises or falls) and in purely speculative bets on market movements.

While hedging activities can obviously be justified in the context of prudent management of a business in a normal commercial environment, they can be seriously harmful where they lead to significant disruption of global commodity or currency markets whose stability is crucial to the welfare of billions of people around the world. Such disruption has been the inevitable result of the massive speculative flows referred to above, particularly where this has also involved deliberate market manipulation by well-financed speculators. Nowhere has this been so evident as in the case of global oil and gas markets, where a series of 'shocks' since 1973 have caused serious economic and social distress, particularly in developing countries. While at times such upheavals have been justly attributed to the actions of the petroleum-exporting countries' cartel, OPEC, this organisation may be said in recent years to have acted more as a stabilising influence in the market, having recognised that it is in their own interests (as well as those of consumers) to avoid sharp fluctuations in prices. Thus, when in the summer of 2008 the world price of crude oil rose by some 75 per cent to $147 a barrel in the space of six months, few sought to blame OPEC. Rather the move was attributed at the time by most commentators to fears of a looming shortage of crude reserves and consequent anticipation of 'peak oil' globally. However, the true culprits – the market speculators and manipulators – were only exposed when the price fell back to $50 by the end of the year. Yet it is striking that, despite the huge damage caused successively to both consumers and producers by these massive gyrations, world leaders did not come under any pressure to reform this grotesquely unstable market structure – another demonstration of the enormous and pernicious power of Wall Street and the global financial establishment.

The profoundly anti-social consequences of leaving the world at the mercy of largely opaque, speculative commodity markets – especially under conditions of global financial deregulation – have been even more dramatically demonstrated in the case of other commodities, particularly foodstuffs. As in the case of oil and gas, world prices of many staples (including rice, maize and wheat) were subject to very sharp increases in 2007–08, followed by steep falls (although these have not necessarily been reflected in a fall in prices to consumers). As also with oil and gas, the most common explanation in the mainstream media for the sharp increases has been supposedly long-term structural factors such as declining productivity of agricultural land and rapid population growth. The much more important role of speculation and market manipulation (intensified as a result of financial liberalisation) – which became obvious once world market prices had fallen back – has been little emphasised and still less considered as in need of restriction.[18] Meanwhile the consequences for developing countries in terms of increased social deprivation and economic disruption – manifest in widespread suicides reported among heavily indebted Indian farmers since 2008 – have been still more severe

---

18. Jayati Ghosh, 'The Unnatural Coupling: Food and Global Finance', April 2009, www.networkideas.org.

than those arising from the fuel price spike (especially given the huge importance of the agricultural sector to their economies).

What makes this man-made disaster and the distorted interpretation of it doubly reprehensible is that it is the all too predictable consequence of the systematic perversion – in line with the Washington Consensus – of the principles of agricultural economics which has been promoted by the World Bank and other donors since the 1990s. Traditionally, these principles have explained, quite correctly, why agriculture needs to be regarded as a special case among economic sectors – in that agricultural markets are naturally prone to extreme cyclical fluctuations in the supply and price of commodities, given (a) the involvement of millions of producers each taking autonomous seasonal decisions on varying the pattern and volume of their output, and (b) the uncertain impact of climate and disease. It was to avoid the damaging consequences of such fluctuations, to producers and consumers alike, that the governments of industrialised countries introduced different forms of market-stabilising intervention schemes after 1945 – which in turn explains why agriculture was excluded from the non-discriminatory trade provisions of the General Agreement on Tariffs and Trade (GATT), largely at the behest of the USA. However, when the GATT was replaced by the World Trade Organization in 1995, it stressed the need to expose agriculture to the principles of non-discriminatory 'free trade' on the same basis as other products, but without offering any explanation for rejecting the earlier rationale for market intervention. By way of compounding this perversion, the industrialised nations – especially the United States and the European Union – have since continued to protect their farm sectors and thereby further distort world agricultural markets while forcing weaker and more vulnerable countries to expose their markets to 'free' competition. The resulting increased market volatility has naturally been a source of intensified social misery across large parts of the developing world, but has been of great benefit to speculative investors chasing ever greater profits.[19]

The 'war' on drugs: a profit-driven perversion of public policy

A future history of the world over the half-century from the 1950s (if the human species survives long enough to write it) may well conclude that the single most bizarre political phenomenon of the period was the virtually uniform commitment of governments around the world to the criminalisation of the production, trading and consumption of narcotic drugs – even to the point where in many countries these activities have been treated as capital offences. Since the 1980s, the US government has even declared itself to be engaged in a 'war' on drugs, to the fighting of which it has devoted vast resources both within and beyond its own territory, including the aerial spraying of coca plantations in South America, (even though locally this is a traditional crop used partly as an antidote to altitude sickness in the Andes) and massive armament shipments to Colombia and Mexico.

What makes the obdurate insistence of the USA and other Western (and Eastern) governments on maintaining this hugely expensive campaign so hard to rationalise is that:

1. Towards the end of the first decade of the new century it is clear that the 'war' has been comprehensively lost, as huge numbers of economically desperate people (particularly in the developing world) have found the trade to be the most attractive, if not the only, way to make a living – consequently

19. See H. Shutt, *A New Democracy: Alternatives to a Bankrupt World Order* (London: Zed Books, 2001), ch. 4.

overwhelming law-enforcement efforts. This tendency has been made all the more pronounced by the fact that indiscriminate globalisation and economic liberalisation – also mandated by the US-led global establishment – has rendered most legal sources of livelihood in poor countries non-viable and has thus led to narcotics becoming the dominant economic sector in many of them, particularly in Africa and parts of Latin America.

2. The USA's own experience of outlawing alcohol (a substance not demonstrably less harmful than marijuana, cocaine or heroin) after World War I should be sufficient proof that pro-hibition is self-defeating.

Yet despite numerous studies detailing the futility and intoler-able costs (social as well as financial) of this policy and frequent denunciations of it in much of the mainstream media,[20] there is a strange reluctance to try to identify the vested interests that have so effectively opposed the ending of prohibition hitherto. In fact it seems self-evident that these must include those groups who benefit from the huge expenditure on prosecuting the 'war' – from enforcement agencies to private-sector prison operators (especially in the USA, where it is estimated that as many as 500,000 people are now in jail for drugs-related offences). An added twist to this notion that the narcotics business might be perceived as a lucrative economic sector by both legal and illegal commercial interests is the suggestion that high growth in consumption – at least among the poorer segment of developed-country populations – may at times have been effectively encouraged by generating high levels of unemployment. In the words of one observer of the heroin culture in Britain in the 1980s (when global heroin use was

---

20. E.g. Clive Crook, 'A Criminally Stupid War on Drugs', *Financial Times*, 13 April 2009.

growing particularly fast) 'the government was basically creating demand'.[21] While such a cynical view might perhaps easily be dismissed, it is plausible to the extent that (a) official attitudes to other forms of vice were becoming more permissive – to the benefit of commercial interests – (see Chapters 1 and 3), and (b) the young unemployed, being without the means to engage in legal forms of consumption, could too easily be induced to form a heroin addiction which they could only afford to feed by engaging in other forms of crime.

Hence it may be that the combination of groups favouring perpetuation of prohibition is akin to the 'military–industrial complex' which is alleged by some to have engineered and sustained the Cold War in order to perpetuate the dominant and lucrative position held by the armaments industry in the USA in the aftermath of World War II.[22] Far more disturbing, but not to be excluded, is the possibility that the policy is effectively dictated by the very organised crime interests that make most money from the drugs business and stand to lose most if decriminalisation were to be implemented, thus driving market prices through the floor.

Such a frightening hypothesis is rendered all the more plausible by the fact that many countries – including ones that are seen as vital in terms of US and Western interests, such as Afghanistan, Colombia and Mexico – have been allowed to reach the point where they are close to becoming 'narco states', in which large parts of the state apparatus, if not the government itself, have

---

21. Irvine Welsh, author of *Trainspotting*, quoted in the *Guardian*, 15 August 2009.

22. See Gore Vidal, 'The Last Empire', *Vanity Fair*, November 1997. It is consistent with this well-known hypothesis to imagine that the wars in Iraq and Afghanistan, which have lasted for most of the first decade of the present century – at a budgetary cost to the USA of at least $1.3 trillion, of which at least 10 per cent is absorbed by private security firms from different countries – have also been sustained if not initiated by profit-seeking interests. See Joseph Stiglitz and Linda Bilmes, 'The Three Trillion Dollar War', *The Times*, 23 February 2008.

fallen under the control of drug barons. For it is scarcely open to doubt that, if only the USA and its allies could be induced to take the logical step of decriminalising narcotics, the prospects for these countries could be immeasurably improved by (a) depriving the criminal and terrorist forces of the income and means to subvert the state and (b) facilitating the provision of greater incentives for legitimate economic activity, particularly for the production of foodstuffs – which could be further encouraged by allowing protection of local markets from the indiscriminate foreign competition that is currently permitted under the irrational hypocrisies of the Washington Consensus (see above).

When on top of this it is understood that US and other Western taxpayers could be saved billions of dollars annually in military support and other costs of fighting this futile 'war', it defies all reason to understand why a truly representative political system would permit it to continue. The only certainty is that whoever is guiding this criminally irresponsible strategy has absolutely no concern to serve the public interest rather than that of their own personal enrichment and is ruthlessly committed to suppressing any authoritative analysis tending to undermine the prohibitionist position, as happened in the case of a damning 1995 World Health Organization report on global cocaine usage that made a strong case for decriminalisation.[23]

The huge controversy surrounding narcotics policy and the suggestion that it may be determined by factors which have nothing to do with advancing the public interest (rather the opposite) serves to emphasise the extent to which debates over public policy are being distorted by the malign influence of private corporate interests in pursuit of maximum profits – as indicated by other case studies presented above. To the extent that this syndrome

---

23. Ben Goldacre, 'Cocaine Study that Got up the Nose of the US', *Guardian*, 13 June 2009.

– which has infected debate over such vital issues as climate change, energy supply, food policy and national security – is now seen to be loading intolerable and unnecessary additional costs (both economic and social) on the community, it may reasonably be concluded that, after a generation of privatisation, it is now time to 'roll back the frontiers' of private profit.

A pattern of resource misallocation

As well as illustrating the abusive diversion of public resources to serve corporate ends, the recurring leitmotif of the various examples of market failure described in this chapter (of which many more could be cited)[24] has been that of wider misallocation of resources. In fact it is a great irony of the profits system that it claims as one of its virtues the tendency to promote the most efficient use of resources – both by channelling investment to the most economically desirable activities and ensuring (through competitive pressures) that the most cost-effective systems of production are applied. Such a claim may seem particularly bizarre in that even many of its defenders recognise, along with J.A. Schumpeter, that it achieves such 'efficient' resource allocation through a process of 'creative destruction', whereby investments are made and obliterated according to a process of Darwinian struggle for market supremacy.

In truth it is counter-intuitive for most people, particularly investors in and employees of businesses threatened with such destruction, that the creation and elimination (in rapid succession) of productive capacity can be equated with economic efficiency. Despite this it remains an article of capitalist faith – notably among ideologues in the Anglo-Saxon world – that this process

---

24. See Shutt, *The Decline of Capitalism*, chs 3 and 4.

is a central benefit of the system. (For them of course there is a compelling logic to maintaining this position, since to abandon it would mean recognising the need for public interference in and regulation of private business.) Yet the negative consequences of the diversion of surplus capital into speculative investment in excess capacity is less and less likely to be acceptable – in an age more conscious of environmental constraints – than it was in nineteenth-century Britain, when the countryside could be littered with inherently unprofitable railways without provoking a national outcry.

This inbuilt propensity for the profits system to misallocate resources therefore seems bound to be viewed as increasingly intolerable as it becomes clearer that the pursuit of high growth is as undesirable as it is futile. By the same token, it must appear completely at odds with an economic ideology (which, as the next chapters will argue, must now emerge in a less growth-oriented world) that is less concerned to serve the priorities of producer interests than the welfare of the mass of ordinary people (individual consumers, workers and taxpayers) as well communities as a whole.

5

A new model:
ending the tyranny of production

THE INSISTENCE OF policymakers in the post-World War II world on making the maximisation of economic growth, as reflected in GDP, the supreme public good in the economic sphere has long been accepted more or less without question by economists and political parties alike. However, as argued in the last two chapters, there are by now compelling reasons for seeing the end of this prioritisation of growth – along with the demise of an enterprise sector driven by profit maximisation – as inevitable.

Such a momentous development in our economic evolution makes it necessary to reconsider the relevance of this supposed indicator of national and global prosperity – which effectively equates prosperity with expanding production as rapidly as possible. In seeking for an alternative to this treadmill of growth and profit maximisation it will be necessary to re-examine some generally held assumptions about the ultimate purpose of economic policy, capitalist or otherwise. These assumptions, it is here suggested, are centred on an implicit belief in the desirability of maximising output which long pre-dates World War II – even though the very concept of GDP, let alone the idea of targeting or maximising its growth, did not exist until the 1930s.

Origins of the expansionist bias

In fact it seems quite natural that there should be a bias in favour of increasing output in any given society. Arguably that is because (a) under traditional economic conditions (before the technological breakthroughs brought about by the agricultural and industrial revolutions of the eighteenth and nineteenth centuries) relative scarcity of commodities was the normal state of affairs in every country; and (b) commercial opportunism would naturally dispose suppliers of goods and services to view increasing output as likely to enhance their living standards and economic security. At the same time governments readily understood the correlation between the level of activity in sectors of the economy which tended to generate most tax revenues and the state of the public finances in an era when preoccupation with the latter – along with concern to protect national trading interests from foreign competition – effectively defined the entire scope of economic policy. This tendency was also linked to a view of international relations (known as mercantilism) which put a premium on maximising exports and minimising imports as a way of assuring a nation's relative economic and military strength vis-à-vis others. Such was broadly the stance of the industrialised countries until about the time of World War I, whereafter extension of the franchise and the consequent creation of welfare states meant that unemployment and social issues became matters of policy concern for the first time.

In terms of the evolution of classical economic theory the most robust expression of this tendency to favour higher output is arguably the so-called 'labour theory of value' as formulated by Ricardo. This theory, according to which the value of a commodity is determined by the amount (and value) of labour used to produce it, is evidently a reformulation of the well-known Say's Law, which states that supply creates its own demand (given the clear presumption that the cost of producing a commodity determines its value irrespective of what value the market – i.e. consumers – might place on it).[1] The obvious implication of this position is that oversupply of markets is not considered to be a realistic threat, at least beyond the short term. Indeed Ricardo's correspondence with his friend and fellow classical economist Malthus makes clear that he differed from the latter in rejecting the idea that excess supply (shortage of demand) could pose a sustained threat to economic stability. Since undoubtedly Malthus's position was more soundly based on empirical evidence, while Ricardo was seemingly unwilling to grasp the dynamics of the business cycle, it may be inferred that the reason Ricardo's view prevailed in terms of the conventional wisdom of the time is that it was seen as more favourable to commercial and business interests.

At all events what is important is that this Ricardian position is the one that has been dominant in relation to the whole theoretical basis of conventional economics ever since the Industrial Revolution. As such it is designed primarily to serve the interests of owners of capital in that

- it prioritises targeting the level of production so as to bring it in line with the available or potential capacity of productive

---

1. Although it is possible to cite passages from Ricardo's writings that indicate he did not actually espouse this rather simplistic theoretical syllogism, there is no doubt that in practice he was ideologically biased in favour of production. The argument in any case tends to be somewhat circular in that it begs the question of what should be the objective basis for valuing labour (both Ricardo and his critics generally related it to the price of corn – i.e. basic subsistence).

factors rather than adjusting capacity to the actual or potential level of consumers' needs or effective demand (this view is reflected in the constant refrain of today's policymakers on the need to close or reduce the 'output gap' between actual production and available capacity);

- it assumes that under conditions of more-or-less free competition markets will always tend to equilibrium at levels consistent with the full employment of productive factors.[2]

Given that this stance was posited on a misplaced implicit belief in the merits of Say's law and the labour theory of value, it may seem hard to explain why it has remained a central part of the corpus of mainstream economic theory even until the twenty-first century. While it is scarcely possible to offer a definitive answer to this conundrum, it may well lie in the emerging balance of political and economic forces in Britain after 1815 – a moment at which the country had reached the apogee of its global supremacy and was at the same time at the forefront of the Industrial Revolution. In fact this may be seen as the culmination of the rise to dominance of the commercial/industrial (Whig) interest since the seventeenth century to a point where it sensed a more or less limitless potential for the global expansion of British capital. In this context Ricardo – who himself epitomised this bourgeois ascendancy as a successful City trader – provided what could be seen as a convenient theoretical framework for the interests he represented. Moreover, the obvious bias of his ideas towards prioritising the maximisation of private profit was merely the reflection of the dominance of this narrow class in what was still a seriously unreformed parliament. What seems more remarkable is that such biased and unrealistic theories have not been permanently discredited in the past two

---

2. Although in reality, as Malthus also pointed out, it was possible for the equilibrium/market clearing price for labour to fall below subsistence level.

hundred years despite the subsequent introduction of universal suffrage and the recognition of more social concerns.

It is true that Keynes recognised the importance of Malthus's critique of Ricardo's simplistic assumptions and endorsed his insight that overproduction was not only possible but chronically inevitable. This was the basis of the important Keynesian stress on the demand side and insistence on the role of state intervention in seeking to bring effective demand in line with latent (underlying) demand. It is notable, however, that Keynes's stance nonetheless endorses the Ricardian assumption that policy should be directed at closing the 'output gap' by expanding demand rather than reducing productive capacity. Indeed this was to become a dominant preoccupation of business leaders and policymakers in the post-World War II era, when it was openly proclaimed that it was necessary to stimulate the continued expansion of consumer demand in the wealthier industrialised countries by artificially creating 'wants'. This was the task of the advertising industry and 'marketing men', whose heyday was the 1950s and 1960s.[3] Such, it may be said, was the basis of the culture of consumerism, which has long been the subject of much criticism but has nevertheless retained a fatal fascination for a large section of the public.

Once the ultimate ineffectiveness of this approach in putting an end to the business cycle had been demonstrated in the 1970s, capitalist economics reverted to crude emphasis on the 'supply side' – even though it was obvious that the long-run inadequacy of demand was the central unresolved problem. The absurd irrationality of this tendency reached its most extreme point in the 1990s when, following the failure of supply-side doctrines to achieve a revival of growth in the 1980s, advocates of the 'new economy' – based on applying 'high-tech' production methods in

3. See J.K. Galbraith, *The Affluent Society* (London: Hamish Hamilton, 1958); André Gorz, *Critique of Economic Reason* (London: Verso, 1989).

electronics and biotechnology – insisted that the resulting rise in productivity would unleash higher rates of growth, ignoring the obvious fact that the consequently increased capacity could only be translated into actual higher output if market demand expanded in parallel.[4]

It is striking that the stress laid on maximising production as a public good, which we have suggested owes much to the influence of Ricardo's theories, has extended beyond the capitalist world. That this is so seems to be largely attributable to the fact that the labour theory of value was adopted by Karl Marx in developing his critique of capitalism. This seems somewhat surprising given Marx's awareness that overinvestment and overproduction were inherent features of the capitalist system, and that this would lead to cyclical depression of market prices. His espousal of this theory appears, in fact, to be linked to his concept of the alienation of labour under industrial capitalism – whereby factory workers had become mere extensions of the machinery (capital) to which they were effectively subordinated and compelled to accept only a marginal share of the value created, whereas Marx held that the workers themselves remained the true source of value.[5] In this he was also expressing a revulsion – which he shared with contemporary critics of industrial capitalism such as John Ruskin and William Morris – at the system's tendency to treat labour as a mere commodity.[6] However, an unfortunate long-term consequence of this philosophical notion was a dogmatic Communist belief in this theory, which was to play a significant part in the

---

4. Alan Greenspan, 'Question: Is There a New Economy?', speech at University of California at Berkeley, 4 September 1998.

5. *Economic and Philosophical Manuscripts* (1844), trans. T.B. Bottomore, in *Karl Marx: Selected Writings in Sociology and Social Philosophy*, ed. T.B. Bottomore and M. Rubel (Harmondsworth: Penguin, 1961).

6. Raymond Williams, *Culture and Society 1780–1950* (London: Chatto & Windus, 1967).

failure of the economic system adopted by the Soviet Union and its satellites. Thus it was normal throughout the Comecon bloc well into the 1980s to find enterprise managers rewarded for maximising their payrolls rather than economising in the use of labour, thereby promoting the opposite of an efficient allocation of resources.

The work fetish

While Ricardo's eccentric theory of value may once have been a convenient prop for official ideologies stressing the primary importance of labour in the economy, it is clear there are other factors behind the political imperative of maximising employment so long espoused by governments in the industrialised world. Central to such ideologies is the idea of the work ethic, which indeed underlies the mores of most societies – particularly in the Western world – from time immemorial and is most famously encapsulated in St Paul's admonition 'if any would not work neither should he eat'.[7] However, in the modern world such values have increasingly run up against a changing economic reality in which, as already noted, the relative scarcity of the means of subsistence has greatly diminished since the Industrial Revolution, while at the same time, because of technological change, the need for labour power per unit of production has also declined.

As pointed out in earlier chapters, the natural consequence of this process over time, in a competitive market, has been a devaluation of labour – and a corresponding increased scarcity of work opportunities. Yet because it remains true that for the vast majority of the world's people the sale of their labour is their only potential source of income, the implications of this long-

---

7. II Thessalonians 3:10.

term downward trend in the demand for and value of labour are startling. It also puts into perspective the rather vague notion of the 'right to work', which was first asserted in the early nineteenth century and is actually enshrined in the 1948 Universal Declaration of Human Rights.[8] In fact, as a number of commentators have observed, this 'right' is a benefit which no society can guarantee and indeed is virtually meaningless for want of any link to a claim to a minimum standard of living – much as the term 'full employment' lacks substance in the absence of any definition of hours and conditions of work. The significance of such an essentially metaphysical claim may therefore perhaps be seen more as an expression of belief in the work ethic – in other words in the duty rather than the right to work. Hence, as has been argued, it is more a reflection of the paternalist ideology of Victorian Poor Law administrators than of any claim of the downtrodden to a basic human right.[9] The same may be said of the once widely held view – often expressed by trade unionists and politicians of the left and enshrined in the famous Beveridge Report on Social Insurance[10] – that unemployment constitutes an indefensible waste of human resources and that such 'enforced idleness' could thus be viewed as a humanitarian crime.

It is self-evident that maintaining the obligation to work in return for entitlement to welfare or other benefits is regarded by governments as a useful lever to keep control and coerce the masses. In a capitalist economy, this is seen by the dominant class as having the added benefit of helping to hold down labour costs by offering what Marx called 'the reserve army of the unem-

---

8. Article 23(1): 'Everyone has the right to work, to free choice of employment, to just and favourable conditions of work and to protection against unemployment.'

9. G. Standing, *Beyond the New Paternalism: Basic Security as Equality* (London: Verso, 2002).

10. *Social Insurance and Allied Services*, Cmnd 6494, November 1942.

ployed' only minimal compensation for being out of work. This spirit has been strongly revived during the present neoliberal era, notably through the adoption in the USA of the Personal Responsibility and Work Opportunity Reconciliation Act by the Clinton administration in 1996. This was a move to substitute the provision of increasingly costly federal welfare payments for the unemployed (introduced under Roosevelt's New Deal in the 1930s) with 'workfare' payments made by state governments only on condition recipients accept work – a principle which the New Labour government has also sought to apply in Britain.

Ironically, however, in the Soviet Union the enslavement of workers to their job or enterprise was far greater, since without such a position individuals stood to lose their homes and all other entitlements – a tradition still reflected today in the former Soviet republics of Central Asia, where the cotton industry still relies on forced labour. This tendency of totalitarian regimes to see enforced labour as a vital instrument of control is also reflected in the Orwellian Nazi slogan *Arbeit macht frei* (Work makes you free).

In fact modern societies, almost regardless of their professed ideology, are inheritors of a historically ingrained assumption that, since work is the only justification for receiving a livelihood, the proper aim of every individual is to acquire a position in which they will be deemed, at least nominally, to be discharging a necessary function or service and thereby earn entitlement to an income. This belief has been reflected in societies as diverse as medieval Europe – where many were reduced to seeking material security by entering religious orders, in which their most valued activity was typically saying prayers for the souls of the dead – and modern industrialised societies (whether notionally capitalist or Communist) where people find paid employment in positions which are not really needed and in which they may pass much of their time attending unnecessary meetings or otherwise 'going through the motions'. Likewise this syndrome has been reflected in the class-based structures designed to reserve particular occupations for particular groups – such as the French aristocracy's monopoly of sinecures under the *Ancien Régime*, the Hindu caste system and Western guilds and professions organised to limit entry and thereby restrict competition and so keep fee rates relatively high. Yet the combination of rapid technological change and intensifying competitive pressures in a stagnant global market are inevitably calling the sustainability of this systematised inefficiency and inequity into question, while at the same time there is ample evidence of increased frustration among the workforce at the combination of futility and insecurity which they now experience at work.[11]

Despite these negative trends, given the controlling attitudes that still prevail at the highest level, there is bound to be strong resistance to any proposals for watering down the traditional link between paid employment and entitlement to an adequate income – even as it is becoming apparent that the availability of meaningful paid jobs is in long-term global decline relative to the size of the labour force (see Chapter 3). Such hostility to change in this relationship is bound to strengthen objections to any kind of recognition that the traditional commitment to pursuing maximum growth will have to be abandoned – even as the need for such a change of priorities becomes ever more pressing – since it would then be impossible to claim that growth would generate sufficient work to eliminate unemployment over time. Yet even now developments in the market are making it more and more difficult to sustain this delusion.

---

11. See C. Maier, *Hello Laziness: Why Hard Work Doesn't Pay* (London: Orion, 2005); Simon Caulkin, 'Why Big Brother Makes an Uneasy Workmate', *Observer*, 13 January 2008.

A continuing squeeze on employment

Ever since the early 1980s, if not before, there has been an intensified tendency for companies to cut staffing levels in response to advances in technology (particularly in microelectronics) permitting increased automation. While the inadequacy of official unemployment data makes it difficult to quantify this trend, there is sufficient anecdotal information – on the scale of corporate downsizing in particular sectors such as banking and telecommunications and the relative decline of the earnings of white-collar staff – to confirm that it is a reality. This position is also consistent with periodic indications of 'jobless growth' in parts of Europe and the long-term decline in average real wages in the USA since the 1970s. At the same time the ease with which layers of middle management can be removed may be reflected in a rising sense of disillusionment among the staff themselves over their status and the relevance of their positions (see below). It needs to be stressed, moreover, that such trends are not confined to the already industrialised countries (see Chapter 3).

Pressure on pension systems

Since the turn of the century pension systems in the industrialised countries have been subject to mounting problems and consequently intensified scrutiny. Most of their difficulties, particularly in the USA and Britain, have arisen because of the failure of private-sector funded schemes, which have been heavily invested in stock markets, to deliver on their 'pension promise' while remaining solvent. This has meant that increasingly their liabilities are being transferred to the state, whether through government-backed insurance schemes assuming responsibility for them directly, or because their failure means that a greater onus for providing pensioners with adequate retirement incomes now falls on public schemes, such as social security in the USA, which are financed through contributions on a pay-as-you-go basis. Consequently it is officially perceived that the overall cost of state pensions, as a proportion of GDP, is set to rise steeply for the foreseeable future – a problem that is aggravated, it is claimed, by the rising longevity of the population, even though this phenomenon has been present for at least a hundred years.

For this reason – and also because of more general constraints to the state budget – it has been determined that the pensionable age for state pension in Britain will need to rise so as to make the basic state pension more affordable (even though the pension level is far lower than in comparable schemes in nearly all other European countries). What is remarkable about this decision is that it has ostensibly been made without considering the dynamic impact the change would have on the labour market. Thus the British government's 2006 White Paper on pensions proposes to raise the retirement age applying to the basic state pension from 65 to 68 – thus adding at least 2 million to the labour force – without any mention of the existing high levels of unemployment but simply stating that 'we will support and encourage extended working lives'.[12] In fact the widespread implicit assumption is that workers who are forced to retire later will simply continue working in their existing jobs – even though this will logically result in blocking promotion or reduced recruitment of younger workers lower down the chain who would otherwise have replaced them.[13] However, when pressed to explain how such a change could be a solution to the problem when it is bound to push up already high rates of unemployment, its advocates are conspicuously silent. All that is

12. 'Security in Retirement: Towards a New Pensions System', Department of Work and Pensions, May 2006.

13. See Jonathan Guthrie, 'When It's Too Expensive to Hang up Your Boots', *Financial Times*, 14 May 2009.

offered by the official propaganda machine is a series of media articles purporting to show that population in developed countries, particularly Europe, is tending to decline and that consequently they will need more workers in future. Such misinformation was the burden of a press release issued in the name of Kofi Annan, United Nations secretary general, in 2004, which even claimed that the population of the European Union was projected to drop from 450 million to 400 million by 2050 – whereas most authoritative estimates indicate it will merely stabilise around the present level – while omitting any mention of the continent's chronically high levels of unemployment.[14]

On the evidence presented thus far it is hard to escape the conclusion that the prevailing economic values of the Western world – inherited as they are from a pre-capitalist era while at the same time indispensable to reinforcing the capitalist ideology – are

1. essentially based upon metaphysical beliefs about the purpose of economic activity and the desirability of work for its own sake;
2. no longer defensible (if they ever were) in relation to the real needs and aspirations of individuals and communities in the modern era – nor, perhaps more importantly, from the perspective of the survival of the human species itself in an increasingly overcrowded and fragile planet.

The new scarcity

It is a familiar notion that economics is essentially the study of scarcity – that is, how to make choices in the allocation or utilisation of scarce resources. In fact, as noted above, the last two hundred years have witnessed unprecedented achievements in vanquishing

---

14. 'Why Europe Needs an Immigration Strategy', United Nations, 29 January 2004, www.un.org/news.

scarcity thanks to a series of technological advances which have vastly increased productivity in agriculture, manufacturing and services. Perhaps the most visible symptom of this achievement is the exponential rise in the world's population, which has grown almost sevenfold since 1850, when it is estimated to have stood at 1 billion – having merely doubled in the previous two centuries.[15] While this growth does not of course mean that material scarcity has ceased to be a constraint facing the majority of the world's people in their daily lives, it does indicate that the technical capacity to support human life has been enormously enhanced.

Paradoxically, however, the very success of the human species in overcoming material scarcity in respect of the supply of goods and services has induced threats of different forms of scarcity that are not necessarily amenable to solution through further technological breakthroughs. Seemingly these do not relate to shortages of natural resources such as petroleum or other minerals – as it was once quite widely believed would be the case – as it has generally been found that technological innovation can ultimately overcome almost any apparent threat of exhaustion of reserves by adapting more abundant substitute materials (such as aluminium for copper) or else by economising in the use of existing ones. On the other hand there are signs that such a finite asset as land – along with vital resources that derive from it such as fresh water and forests – is threatened with permanent damage or depletion because of overpopulation and overuse (in some cases exacerbated by mass poverty, as in the case of the deforestation for domestic fuel in many parts of Africa and Asia, where many people cannot afford or do not have access to electricity or other more modern sources of energy). Equally, in more prosperous areas land scarcity relative to high population density – combined with high consumption levels

---

15. Figures cited in Fernand Braudel, *The Structures of Everyday Life*, volume 1 of *Civilisation and Capitalism, 15th–18th Century* (London: Collins, 1981).

– can lead to unacceptable loss of amenity (e.g. through traffic congestion) or damage to health through pollution.

At the same time a different and less reversible type of scarcity has emerged in the shape of a shortage of employment opportunities for the world's still rising population. As suggested earlier, this is primarily a function of rising productivity driven by technological change. As such, it is a consequence of the very forces that have served to eliminate the more traditional scarcities and that have been displacing labour ever since the Industrial Revolution. It is an ironic outcome to this process of human scientific advancement that the negative consequences of overpopulation should have combined with the supposedly liberating ones of increased human productiveness to threaten greater mass impoverishment. Yet this is precisely the phenomenon that is tending to undermine the struggle of regions such as South and East Asia to generate enough jobs for their still growing populations.[16]

A more rational ideology

Desperate efforts to divert public attention from these realities with misinformation – and thereby sustain irrational beliefs and values – can only postpone the need to confront reality, which will become totally inescapable once it is accepted that targeting the maximisation of growth must be ended. In that event a more rational, sustainable and politically acceptable economic model will need to be developed which shifts the emphasis away from prioritising the interests of producers (owners of capital and labour) – including the insatiable demand to devote an ever greater share of value-added to maintaining the rate of return on accumulated capital – towards giving primacy to the interests

16. William Pesek, 'Climate Change Threatens Asia's Future Growth', *Bloomberg News*, 5 May 2009.

of the far greater number of consumers and taxpayers (many of whom are also of course workers). This will obviously also mean abandoning the manifestly irrational attempt to try to force an ever larger proportion of the population to compete for increasingly non-existent jobs.

In such a 'post-Ricardian' world people should have the chance better to respond to what should surely be the basic purpose of a rational economic system: *to provide people with what they need and want to the maximum extent permitted by the available resources.* (This might be seen as consistent with the old Utilitarian ideal of 'the greatest happiness of the greatest number'.) The starting point for finding ways to realise this goal in the modern world must be to recognise that

1. work (in the sense of supplying a marketable product or service) should not necessarily be the principal determinant of a citizen's entitlement to an income;
2. time spent in paid employment (or self-employment) as a proportion of each adult lifespan is bound to continue shrinking – as a function of both technology-induced increases in labour productivity and steadily rising longevity.

Acceptance of these presumptions would be the essential key to escaping the otherwise insoluble problems of the scarcity of jobs while at the same time providing the opportunity to create and enjoy more varied and fulfilling lifestyles than most people have been able to imagine. Thus a positive consequence of the combination of vastly increased productivity and the restrictions imposed on economic activity by a finite planet should be the realisation of the vision of those critics of industrial capitalism[17] who have insisted that work should either be a pleasurable, crea-

17. William Morris, *How We Live and How We Might Live* (1884).

tive activity or, where it cannot be of this kind, as little time as possible should be spent upon it.

Such a development would also facilitate concrete recognition by society of the many family 'carers' who look after children and the elderly or disabled without any formal wage or definition of their hours and conditions of work – whose hugely important contribution to the welfare of society is thus not captured in GDP. The potential economic benefits – as well as the social justice – of providing material reward for these and other 'voluntary' activities of value to society are spelt out in the next chapter.

However, it should be obvious that, while such a new economic order would in principle offer much greater scope for the population in general to fulfil their individual and collective aspirations – and thus be liberating for the vast majority – it would be far from libertarian in the economic sense. Indeed, bearing in mind the seeming long-term trend to greater scarcity of land and other finite resources relative to a still expanding world population, there will be a premium on both halting (if not reversing) population growth and on minimising waste and misallocation of resources. This will be further grounds for welcoming the prospective marginalisation of the profit motive, given its enormous propensity to promote such waste (so copiously illustrated in Chapter 4). By the same token, given that the primacy of the profit motive is very much causally linked to the persistence of the capitalist business cycle, its marginalisation will have another obvious benefit: in reducing or even eliminating the chronic instability and insecurity arising from its otherwise unavoidable cyclical fluctuations.

For these reasons, as will be made clear in the next chapter, a more soundly based economic order would impose significant restraints on the acquisitiveness of individuals or groups in relation to the finite opportunities for material self-enrichment that would be available.

6

Evolving a more rational
economic system

IN ATTEMPTING TO define the shape of a more functional and tolerable economic model such as could conceivably emerge from the wreckage of the collapsed profits system, this work starts from the presumption that it is still possible to imagine its being an evolutionary rather than a revolutionary process. Whether or not this is realistic – which may well be doubted in view of the continuing refusal of any mainstream political parties or media in the industrialised world to contemplate any meaningful change to the neoliberal status quo – it would in any event be still more unrealistic to put forward a blueprint for a post-capitalist order on the basis that it could be imposed in a vacuum in the aftermath of a total breakdown of global order (or even world war). In this spirit of cautious optimism the present chapter seeks to define the essential elements of a viable economic order for the future.

Basic strategic orientation

The long-term aim must be to ensure *stability* consistent with securing minimum adequate living standards for all. Given the implication that growth will be limited – ideally on a world scale – this will entail significant income redistribution, both within countries and between rich and poor countries. The latter would in fact need to experience significant growth in GDP (per head of population) as a result of this process – although this would not in itself be seen as a measure of rising prosperity as much as would certain social indicators (for example, more even income distribution, minimum average intake of calories per head and access to sanitation).

Although for industrialised countries it would not be a specific target of public policy to expand national income (GDP) – as conventionally measured – it would be important for all countries to sustain it at a minimum level. This is because GDP is an indicator of the aggregate level of value-added within a given economy and, as such, reflects the level of activity in the cash economy and of personal income and livelihoods being generated in a given period. Hence if this aggregate were allowed to fall significantly over time it would mean that, collectively, domestic enterprises, workers and the wider community would be worse off in terms of disposable cash income, which in turn would weaken the overall national economy by reducing the resource (and tax) base at its disposal. For this reason it would also be important for any country – particularly poor ones with a small existing tax base – to be able to shield their economies against either predatory competition from abroad or significant flows of funds out of the country, both of which would tend to diminish the value-added remaining to be deployed within the national community.

A more rational globalisation

For the purposes of formulating the alternative model to be outlined in this chapter it is assumed that the structure of international organisation will remain broadly as it is for the foreseeable future, in that

- legal authority will continue to be vested primarily in the governments of nation-states responsible for determining policies and laws within their respective territories;
- representative international bodies will be empowered both to regulate economic relations between nation-states and to facilitate measures aimed at redressing undue imbalances in wealth and income between them.

While it is taken as given that maximum economic cooperation and integration between nation-states is essential, it is also seen as equally important that a large degree of autonomy be retained at national level – and indeed at local level within national economies. This is in line with the principle that different local communities should be enabled to have the maximum degree of autonomy consistent with international collective security and stability. However, to the extent that there would be an attempt to coordinate national growth strategies in the context of a broad target of international GDP stability, forums will need to be established to facilitate this despite the obvious impediments to effective harmonisation. It is important to stress that, in order to promote such harmonisation and at the same time foster general economic collective security, the formation and strengthening of regional groupings of states – such as the European Union – would be encouraged.

What will manifestly be quite untenable under the new order is the perpetuation of the present liberalised pattern of regulation which constitutes the essence of what is known as globalisation. Most obviously this is because

1. in a world where it is explicitly accepted that growth maximisation is no longer a desirable objective of public policy – and

where scarcity is likewise recognised as a reality – the role of the 'free' market in allocating wealth and resources between different countries and groups will have to be tempered by official intervention so as to ensure equitable income distribution;

2. different national (and indeed local) communities will only be able to assure equitable and stable levels of income and economic activity within their jurisdiction if they have effective control over matters such as taxation rates, public finance and standards governing labour and the environment – which in turn depends on their having power to limit the free movement of capital, thereby escaping from the 'race to the bottom'.

It would arguably be preferable for the problems associated with globalisation to be resolved through international agreements on harmonisation of rules and regulations. However, while such harmonisation is certainly a desirable goal in any case, it would be dangerously utopian to assume this could be achieved in a time frame of less than one or two decades and without considerable defaulting by individual states – as suggested by the climate-change negotiations under the Kyoto Protocol. Hence it would be vital in the meantime to restore some publicly accountable control over domestic economic management. In order to do this there would be no substitute for taking steps to bring back effective controls on the movement of capital into and out of national jurisdictions. The extent and nature of these controls could naturally be varied according to the perceived needs of each country's authorities. However, it should be stressed that in order to be effective they must be consistently administered and combined with other measures to regulate trade and encourage enterprise, following the example of East Asian countries such as South Korea and China. Failing this they may simply serve to promote a parallel foreign currency market and a black economy (beyond the reach of the tax authorities), as has too often happened in the past in other developing countries, notably in Africa. Indeed such experience suggests the strong desirability of promoting currency integration on a regional basis among the smallest and financially weakest developing countries as the indispensable condition of their acquiring a greater degree of economic self-determination.[1] A potentially important initiative along these lines has been the launch of the Bank of the South in 2006 by president Hugo Chávez of Venezuela with the support of the governments of Argentina, Bolivia, Ecuador and other South American countries, while a similar approach has been proposed for Asia by the leader of the Democratic Party of Japan, elected to power in August 2009.

Restoring monetary order

In fact the need to re-establish greater currency stability – nearly forty years after the post-war Bretton Woods system of more or less fixed exchange rates was abandoned – will be crucial to bringing the presently anarchic pattern of globalisation under control. Ideally this would involve the creation of an international unit of account – whose value would be fixed in terms of a basket of commodities (including gold and other metals) over which no country or group of countries could command a disproportionate share – as the central reserve currency against which the value of all others would be set. The issue and administration of this reserve currency would need to be entrusted to an international body which was genuinely representative of all countries (or regional economic/currency blocs) rather than the United States or any other dominant power. While the resolution of this vexed question will not be easy or quick, it is clear that the status quo

---

1. See Shutt, *A New Democracy*, ch. 7.

– under which the US dollar remains the sole reserve currency, despite no longer having any tangible backing – cannot endure much longer, particularly as the US economy weakens relative to the rest of the world. Any change will nonetheless be strongly resisted, not only by the US government, whose power is enormously enhanced by the status quo, but by the currency trading industry, which stands to suffer a sharp reversal of the sixfold growth of the foreign exchange market since 1988 (reaching some $4 trillion daily by 2008).

It should be noted, however, that the general abandonment of growth should greatly improve the chances of achieving international currency stability, bearing in mind that the pressure to maintain and enhance high growth rates – in a competitive world environment – was a principal cause of the collapse of the Bretton Woods system. In the absence of such pressures and with the benefit of greater restraints on profit maximising and risk taking by currency traders, the balance of forces should increasingly favour greater exchange-rate stability in future.

The role of enterprise

As already made clear, the necessary commitment of governments to long-term strategies based on minimal rates of GDP growth will be fatal to the rationale of the profit-maximising corporation, which has been the central focus of the model of economic organisation that has been in place in the industrialised world since the first British companies' legislation was enacted around 1860.[2] For, as is well known from the history of the profits system in the period since then (as described in earlier chapters), once companies can no longer expand through the organic growth of their existing

---

2. Including the Limited Liability Act 1855, and the Companies Act 1862.

businesses the surplus profits they unavoidably accumulate can have only two possible outlets: either (a) the acquisition of other companies or (b) the buying and selling of corporate or other assets in pursuit of purely speculative profits. Equally, however, history demonstrates that both these outlets inevitably run into the brick wall of systemic overcapacity and financial collapse, as confirmed yet again by the current 'neoliberal' crisis which has been inexorably unfolding since the late 1980s if not before.

For defenders of the existing system the best hope must be that, as in past crises, the ultimate outcome will be a return to 'business as usual' following a destruction of capital which they must pray will not meanwhile engulf most of the existing corporate sector. Yet even they must wonder whether such a process will be politically acceptable or achievable without unleashing a global holocaust of misery and violence among the hundreds of millions of people whose lives will be ruined in consequence – or, in the case of billions more in the developing world, made even more intolerable than they already are. However, as suggested earlier, because of the growing redundancy of capital resulting from continued rapid technological change, it must be doubtful in any event whether the demand for investment capital will ever again be sufficient to make a sustained revival of stock markets a realistic possibility. Indeed, as suggested in Chapter 3, the same forces are putting traditional business models under strain, perhaps portending the terminal decline of many established corporations in any event.

On the more realistic assumption that such a resurrection of the status quo/pre-crisis model proves unattainable it must follow that more and more private businesses will collapse as the global economy fails to recover. In that event it seems inevitable that many of those enterprises that do not disappear as a result will fall into de facto public ownership by default, and will in consequence need to be managed under state supervision indefinitely, except to the extent that they could be hived off to non-profit organisations – such as community companies (see below) with a strong interest in supporting them to the benefit of their local economy. In such a context, where there will be little possibility of selling them back to the private sector as going concerns, it will be necessary for governments to formulate criteria for the management of such businesses under conditions that will enable them to survive – as long as this is perceived to be viable in terms of the public interest – but will preclude any prospect of their returning to levels of profitability sufficient to attract private investment. Such a necessity, it should be noted, has not been felt in respect of the banks and other financial institutions which have been taken into majority state ownership by the US and British governments since September 2008; rather it has been pronounced that these organisations will continue to be managed on the same basis as previously (and often by the same executives), with the avowed intention of returning them to full private ownership as soon as feasible.[3] Given the firm public commitment of the Anglo-Saxon countries to the neoliberal agenda – which strongly favours private over public ownership on principle – such a stance is understandable. Yet it seems doubtful whether such knee-jerk refusal to face the reality of long-term market weakness and consequent corporate unprofitability – of which there have already been signs in the performance of stocks over the past decade (see Chapter 3) – will be sustained for long as the truth dawns.

Once this gloomy long-term prospect for corporate profitability is seen to be linked to an inevitable downgrading of growth as a public priority it is bound to be recognised that an entirely different regime is required for the corporate sector from the one

---

3. Along with General Motors, taken into public ownership in May 2009.

currently prevailing. The need for this is likely to seem all the more compelling as public awareness grows of the substantial costs to the public arising from the increasingly anti-social activities of the private corporate sector, largely facilitated by the combination of lax regulation, state subsidy and ultimate underwriting of profitability, stimulating ever greater orgies of moral hazard and inevitably ending in financial disasters such as that which has been unfolding since 2007. Indeed it is hard to believe – notwithstanding the continued barrage of official propaganda as to the huge 'wealth-creating' benefits of the profit motive – that public opinion will not finally revolt against the damage wreaked on the economy and society by its distorting impact, leading to misinformation and perversion of debate on vital issues of public policy (see Chapter 4) and ever greater misallocation and waste of scarce resources.

In light of the above prognosis a more functional and publicly acceptable pattern of enterprise organisation would have the following characteristics:

1. *Corporate accountability*. Companies would, as a matter of law, only be able to benefit from (a) limited liability, (b) state investment in the form of equity or loan capital (or guarantees) or (c) discriminatory subsidies or tax breaks on condition that the community was effectively represented on their boards of directors with power to veto or set conditions to board decisions in the public interest – or else that the company was constituted on a non-profit basis. The purpose of this provision would be to ensure that (i) the companies would be able to enjoy such privileges only where it was perceived that it would serve a specific public purpose (such as development or promotion of a particular product), (ii) any profits accruing to shareholders would be limited to a level equal to a return on their investment of little more than the rate of inflation. Given

such restrictions on potential returns to shareholders, it seems unlikely that many private investors would wish to put their money into such heavily community-influenced companies, given the implicitly high risk of loss relative to the prospective rewards.

2. *Enterprise ownership and management.* In general non-profit ownership of enterprises would be encouraged, such that any profits beyond limited amounts to be retained for organic development of the business (to be agreed by democratic decision) would be distributed annually to shareholders, members, employees or taxpayers. It could be on the basis of full public ownership – at national or local (e.g. municipal) level – or mutual or cooperative structures. (Existing examples of these include community interest companies in Britain[4] and municipally owned *Stadtwerke* in Germany – see also Chapter 7). It would of course need to be ensured that appropriate legal frameworks exist to provide transparent accountability. Joint stock (shareholder) companies on the current model could still exist but would do so in an increasingly unfavourable environment. Thus it would still be legally possible for privately owned companies to operate independently, although they would be discouraged from accumulating profits – perhaps through tax incentives to distribute these to shareholders (quite the opposite of the capital allowances currently available to them as an incentive to reinvestment of profits). In these circumstances it may well be imagined that many shareholders would feel themselves as marginalised by public-sector representatives, as they already do by boards of directors and management under the existing model, with the result that they will rapidly become an endangered species.

---

4. Established under the terms of the Companies Act 2004.

3. *Market signals.* While the market would continue to have a role in determining the allocation of resources, the latter would be much more strongly influenced than hitherto by wider economic considerations such as the environment (biosphere). Decisions as to the level of output of given commodities would thus need to balance the aim of meeting demand in full (even at the risk of temporary oversupply) against concern to avoid wasteful use of resources. Likewise the general principle would be that prices of goods and services should reflect full economic costs.

4. *Regulation and competition control.* Given the presumption that growth will be restricted and consequently that individuals' ability to appropriate economic value-added will have to be limited on an equitable basis, there will be a bias against competition, particularly in sectors where this could lead to the substantial loss of activity and value-added in a given area, thus potentially destabilising the local economy and community. However, in the absence of the competitive spur to maintaining cost-effective operation of enterprises it would be necessary to put in place other mechanisms to achieve this purpose. These might consist of a sector regulator empowered to supervise companies and make recommendations on performance, costs and quality combined with the development of a set of norms to be applied by firms operating in each sector. The criteria to be applied would also include that of maximum economic efficiency (long-term lowest economic cost[5]) and minimum waste of resources. Likewise, application of common minimum standards in respect of labour and the environment should be legally enforceable in respect of all enterprises.

---

5. This means taking account of all 'externalities' not normally accounted for in commercial cost–benefit calculations (e.g. environmental damage, loss of amenity to the public/consumers).

Income distribution and employment

Since it would only be possible, under a regime of minimal growth, to employ a limited and progressively dwindling proportion of the labour force on a full-time basis (as conventionally understood[6]) it would make no sense to continue a policy of maximising the utilisation of labour. By the same token, given that it would no longer be remotely possible to claim that everyone would be able, in an uncontrolled labour market, to have an equal opportunity to maximise their incomes by working full time, it would be hard to defend a highly skewed distribution of income such as is currently tolerated in Britain, the USA and many other countries, particularly in the developing world. Assuming that employment (or self-employment) were to remain the principal determinant of personal income levels, it follows that some approach to effective rationing of earning opportunities would need to be incorporated in the regulation of the labour market, while a significant reduction in the gap between the highest and lowest rates of pay would also be necessary. At the same time a progressive income tax could be used to achieve more even income distribution.

If at the same time, out of respect for the long-standing obsession with obliging everyone to work for a living, it were still thought necessary to try to include all adults in the active labour force, it would be found that average working time would have to be drastically shortened – and progressively so on the reasonable assumption that labour productivity would continue to rise in response to technological advance. In theory this could be done by cutting the length of either the average working week, working year or working life – or perhaps a combination of all three. At a certain point, however, it may well appear to be less

---

6. That is, working at least 1,700–2,000 hours annually for a period of 35–40 years.

than optimally efficient to employ two or more people to fill a position which could be quite adequately covered by one on what is at present considered a full-time basis. This would apply particularly to those skilled occupations (such as medical specialists, for example) where training costs are relatively high.

In practice, taking all the above factors into consideration, it seems likely there will be no clear-cut solution to this conundrum – and that norms would only be established as a result of an evolutionary process responding to the unforeseeable dynamics of different labour markets. Rather, in the first instance these markets would be regulated on the basis of the following guiding principles:

1. an indicative maximum number of working hours per week/ year would be established as the norm for full-time employment of any individual, but with provision for exceptions in special cases;
2. no unnecessary work should be undertaken – or jobs created – simply in order to provide a means of income distribution;
3. no group (such as a professional institute) would have the right to determine the numbers of those accredited to undertake a particular occupation or the applicable levels of remuneration without reference to a representative public body charged with regulating levels of employment or approving pay structures;
4. governments should explicitly jettison the ever more meaningless goal of 'full employment' – presently used to justify support for maximising growth.

This change of emphasis would clearly imply a need to revisit the traditional work ethic and culture – see Chapter 7. What would clearly be inescapable would be the establishment of a radically different system of income distribution.

Basic income – an idea whose time has come

Given the necessary abandonment of any commitment by governments to facilitate the provision of jobs, let alone to try to achieve
'full employment', it would be politically unavoidable to offer some
form of minimum income guarantee to all. This should be based
on universal entitlement to a basic or citizen's income (at a flat
basic 'survival' level) regardless of means or employment status. In
principle this should remove the threat of income poverty from all
adults and with it the social problems and distortions of the labour
market that result from the competitive struggle to find employment in order to achieve minimum material security. This concept
has been under consideration in different political and academic
circles – of both left and right – around the world at least since
the 1980s,[7] but has yet to be implemented on a universal basis in
any country. Although different variants have been proposed, the
essential features are

1. a flat-rate payment as of right to all resident citizens over the
   school leaving age, irrespective of means or employment status;
2. it would in principle replace all existing social-security entitlements with the exception of child benefits (payable in
   respect of those under the school leaving age) and with special
   supplementary allowances for the infirm and disabled – as well
   as for otherwise unpaid family carers looking after them.[8]

Opinions among advocates of this concept vary as to (a) how
far payments should be totally unconditional or subject (for example) to some token community service, (b) what would be

---

7. Notably through the Basic Income Earth Network (BIEN), www.basic-income.org.
8. Basic state pensions would also be subsumed under the basic income entitlement; however, additional age-related benefits or targeted support for those with special needs would also be required.

the appropriate level of benefit relative to other incomes and/or basic subsistence costs, and (c) how it should be financed. While no attempt can be made here to establish definitive norms in respect of these issues, it may be mentioned that an estimate of the net cost of providing such a universal basic income in Britain in 2009 would be equivalent to around 28 per cent of GDP and an average (flat) income tax rate of 57 per cent – around double the current basic rate of tax and national insurance.[9] However, while this tax estimate makes some allowance for the substantial administrative cost savings that would result from the abandonment of means testing, it takes no account of other possible sources of expenditure saving (e.g. on job creation schemes or projects that would no longer be justified) or of tax-revenue sources such as the substantial ones that could be generated from that part of existing national value-added that would no longer be required to service accumulated excess capital and debt on corporate balance sheets (see below).

As against this, however, it is important to stress the conspicuous benefits that a basic income scheme would offer:

- The replacement of all existing social-security benefits (e.g. unemployment benefit) and elimination of means-testing would not only bring large savings in administrative costs (see above) but at the same time remove the 'poverty trap' associated with means-tested benefits, which at present means that the marginal cost of moving off benefit into employment can be prohibitive.
- Liberating large numbers of people from the treadmill of unnecessary and soul-destroying 'work' would allow them to

---

9. Citizen's Income Trust (UK), *Newsletter*, no. 3, 2009. This assumes that existing personal allowances and tax reliefs on pension contributions would be withdrawn and thus credited back to the tax base.

pursue more fulfilling and creative lives without necessarily generating a cash reward from it – thus permitting an end to the 'commodification' of labour (see Chapter 5). By the same token this would allow people to participate in more activities on a voluntary basis as part of non-profit organisations which might be of intangible (socio-economic) benefit but which otherwise would not be undertaken.

- Ending the need for government to create jobs would lead not only to further large fiscal savings but the elimination of the often wasteful misallocation of scarce resources on schemes with no lasting economic benefit (see Chapter 4).

It is notable also that – in a climate where both non-profit enterprise and economy in the use of resources were to be officially encouraged – the absence of any artificial incentive to create jobs would further reinforce the general bias against waste. This would mean, for example, that energy companies would feel less disincentive to promote conservation by their customers rather than increased consumption, while recycling of used goods would not necessarily be seen as spoiling the market for new production (e.g. the supply of second-hand clothes to the poor) and associated employment. By the same token there would be little incentive to stimulate increased demand – whether through 'planned obsolescence' of products (from motor cars to computer software) or by artificially creating wants – in order to close the 'output gap', which would become a largely irrelevant concept.

Disputes over determination of income distribution would persist but would have to be resolved through a different, non-market dynamic because of recognition that not all could necessarily have access to employment; thus rewards would need to be determined largely through collectively agreed scales of value rather than competitive market forces. This would clearly imply a tendency to greater equality of reward within the community, since the aggregate amount of value-added (income) to be distributed would be limited.

Equally, given that the requirement to maximise returns to shareholders would be removed – along with the bias in favour of the most capital-intensive forms of fixed investment – it would become apparent that a substantial share of economic value-added that is at present wastefully diverted to serving the priorities of the owners of capital could be more usefully devoted to financing the Citizen's Income and serving the economic priorities of the wider public. This share comprises mainly what is presently appropriated as profit or debt service on the existing stock of private equity and loan capital – which may well amount to as much as 15 per cent of GDP in the USA and Britain[10] – but also the huge sums diverted to economically inefficient public infrastructure projects whose main purpose is to provide an outlet for reinvestment of excess profits.[11]

An end to the anarchy of the global 'free' market

It has been made clear why, under an economic model based on restricted growth, it will be necessary to limit competition and regulate enterprise within national economies. By the same token, because of the need to ensure equitable access to relatively static (or slowly growing) global value-added, cross-border trade and capital flows would need to be regulated by international agreement – so that globalisation would cease to be a 'race to the bottom' for all countries. Self-evidently, this implies that trade

---

10. See Shutt, *The Decline of Capitalism*, pp. 126–7.
11. E.g. the British government's profoundly perverse recent decisions to support investment in uneconomic and anti-environmental projects such as the massive expansion of nuclear power generation and the construction of a third runway at Heathrow Airport.

flows must as far as possible be managed with a bias in favour of the poorest countries, so that they can be enabled to close the gap in living standards with the industrialised nations. This would mean not only allowing them to provide their producers of goods and services with adequate protection against imports but providing them with sufficient affordable finance and other support to establish cost-effective production capacity (with sufficient safeguards against inefficiency and corruption) – see Chapter 8.

In any event it seems quite likely that, out of concern for the environment and the threat of global warming, there will in future be a greater premium on sourcing goods from domestic or regional producers so as to reduce the 'carbon footprint' of international freight transport. Hence, taken together with the granting of greater latitude to individual countries in protecting domestic markets, there would be a substantial decline in both volume and value of international trade. Such a development, it may be remarked, would amount to the discrediting of another much-cherished shibboleth of the classical economists, the belief that the maximisation of trade is a public good. In fact this notion – enshrined in the classical theory of international trade based on 'comparative advantage' – is essentially another eighteenth-century fetish (alongside that of labour) sanctified by Ricardo and derived from the same Whig ideology biased in favour of increased production and commerce (see Chapter 5).

Under this new orientation of the global trade system the World Trade Organization would have a totally different role and its existing rules would need to be replaced. Instead of purporting to promote non-discriminatory market access to member countries the new rules would accept the reality of discrimination and focus on seeking to minimise the potential for undue distortion or disruption to trade and economic activity that could be caused by bilateral or multilateral agreements. It could also be given the role

– in conjunction with other UN agencies – of promoting greater harmonisation of standards in respect of treatment of labour, the environment and taxation.

Commodity and currency markets

The hugely damaging impact of the present largely unregulated world markets for vital raw materials and foodstuffs – especially where speculators are allowed to manipulate prices with the sole purpose of maximising their own profits – has been described in Chapter 4. In order to prevent, or at least severely curtail, such activities support should be given to publicly managed price stabilisation mechanisms designed to balance the interests of producers and consumers. In the case of essential foodstuffs, countries would be encouraged to establish domestic stocks based on guaranteed minimum prices and quotas to registered farmers (so as to prevent excess supply and hold down costs). For these and other major internationally traded commodities – notably petroleum and petroleum products – market stabilisation mechanisms (managed by publicly funded and accountable agencies of the UN) will need to be established with an explicit mandate to intervene in world markets so as to stabilise prices – within a range to be fixed annually or seasonally – taking proper account of the interests of both producers and consumers. Such institutions would be preferable to cartels representing producers only, such as OPEC. In addition to such rationalised market intervention supervision of international commodity exchanges – by public bodies that are ultimately answerable to the world community as a whole – must be assured so as to prevent damaging manipulation of prices in the sole interest of a few private speculators.

The equally harmful effects of uncontrolled global currency markets will also need to be brought in check in the interests of greater economic stability. As suggested above, the primary mechanism for achieving this should be the re-establishment of a regime of more or less fixed parities akin to that which existed under the Bretton Woods system up to 1971. Yet, as in the case of the similar approach suggested for stabilising commodities markets, such reforms will be bitterly resisted by the organised lobby of market traders – who continue to make enormous profits from this speculative trade precisely because of the enormous volatility that is so harmful to the vast majority.

Tax evasion

Even many vocal supporters of globalisation have come to recognise that one of its more negative consequences is to promote both tax competition among different countries struggling to attract or retain investment and outright tax evasion via the numerous tax havens created round the world in order to attract both honestly and dishonestly acquired funds. Hence there can be no justification whatever for allowing these pockets of legalised criminality to remain in existence under a reformed world order. In those territories where their establishment has been encouraged because there is supposedly no alternative form of activity to constitute the local economic base (as in many small island colonies and former colonies of Britain and other European countries) it must be recognised that the price of maintaining such tiny and inherently uncompetitive communities in existence at all is inevitably a significant measure of de facto subsidy from outside.

Criteria for public choice

As already indicated, the guiding principle for designing a more acceptable global economic order should be to enable individuals and communities to fulfil their desires and aspirations consistent with what is feasible within the limits of available resources.

Crucially, this would mean that decisions on the allocation of such resources would be based on criteria of (a) informed public choice as between different options (e.g. a hospital versus a sports stadium; development of treatments for prostate cancer rather than HIV), and (b) maximum cost-effectiveness of resource use in relation to both investment in (construction) and implementation or operation of any given programme or facility.

In line with these criteria – and in keeping with the commitment to end the prioritisation of GDP growth as a public good – no project would be undertaken on the basis that it was intended to increase utilisation of either capital or labour, or indeed of any other resource. This approach could thus be seen as the negation of the Keynesian 'pump-priming' principle, whereby the implementation or expansion of projects is seen as largely a means of stimulating the overall level of activity through 'multiplier' effects. Likewise people would no longer be encouraged to spend their incomes or consume for the sake of boosting production of goods or services and increasing utilisation of productive capacity, thereby giving the lie to the Keynesian notion of the 'paradox of thrift' – a fallacy of economic theory seeking to justify excessive and wasteful consumption and investment. It is thus a final irony that, with the de-emphasis on growth maximisation and downgrading of the profit motive – always claimed by its champions to be the optimal mechanism for achieving efficient allocation of resources – it would at last be possible to end the perverse incentives to waste of resources which have long been such a conspicuous reality of modern capitalism,[12] and thus move towards

---

12. Such as the car scrappage schemes instituted in many industrialised countries in 2009 (designed to induce people to bring forward replacement of their existing vehicles) with a view to offsetting the vast excess capacity in the global motor industry.

minimising their use in an age when conservation will be at an ever higher premium.

Such a commitment to economy in the use of scarce resources would also call for a reversal of what have earlier been identified as two of the most perversely damaging policy stances adopted by the global establishment in the late capitalist era. This would entail:

1. The decriminalisation of narcotic drugs – that is, putting their supply and use on the same (licensed) basis as alcohol and tobacco. While it is hard to quantify the net financial savings that would result – huge savings in terms of law enforcement and imprisonment of convicts, to be partly offset by the increased resources devoted to treatment of addiction – they would be far exceeded by the immeasurable social cost savings in terms of human suffering of those, particularly addicts, so pointlessly criminalised at present. (At the same time, however, it would be necessary, particularly in developing countries where this industry has become so economically important, to ensure adequate support and protection for alternative sources of livelihood, notably in agriculture.)

2. An explicit official commitment to curbing population growth – with the aim of achieving stability of the world population in, say, thirty years. This would require tangible support – including the subsidised provision of contraceptives – by major UN agencies for family-planning programmes in those (mainly developing) countries where growth rates are highest.

7

Ideology for the twenty-first century:
cooperation, creativeness, equality

As set out in the previous chapter, the elements of the more rational economic society that must emerge from the presently disintegrating one dominated by profit-maximising capitalism are determined largely by the need to bring order out of chaos. The recognition of this need in turn derives from a perception that the present system has become not only outmoded and hopelessly dysfunctional in terms of its impact on human society but unsustainably destructive of the biosphere on a finite planet.

Logically, however, what should emerge from this shift of emphasis is not simply a more rational form of consumer society but one in which people would be encouraged not just to limit their consumption but to express their individuality and talents by other means. While this may strike some as utopian, it is evident that, in a world where the physical and practical constraints to pursuing growth maximisation are accepted, such non-materialist aspirations will need to be encouraged – and indeed adopted – if the human species is to survive. For given that the size of aggregate value-added (GDP) is assumed to remain more or less static over time, restraints on the ability of individuals to capture more than a certain share of the total will need to be put in place. While this will not mean seeking to attain absolute equality of rewards, it would clearly involve a severe curtailment of the huge disparities in income currently prevailing in most countries (as well as between them). At the same time, it would be vital to foster a spirit of mutual cooperation and solidarity in place of the Darwinian competitiveness that is inherent in market capitalism. This may prove easier to the extent that there is already evidence of growing popular disenchantment with the ideology of profit maximisation and the commodification of people and of ever more aspects of life in general (see below).

But if it is now plain that the welfare of the human race can no longer be advanced by the perpetual, competitive pursuit of profit and expansion of output, it will be necessary that the more stable global economic order outlined in the last chapter should be driven by a more positive ideology than one of simply minimising harm. While it is hard to define *a priori* what this might be, it may be hoped that it will be found in the possibilities for individual self-expression and collective endeavour in a world where people will feel progressively less in thrall to the struggle for material survival, so that they will be better able to engage in a process of self-discovery while taking advantage of the more benign potential of technological change.

It is apparent that, in order to adapt to the demands and constraints of a no-growth or low-growth economy, human society will need to undergo a significant change in attitudes. In fact, as indicated below, it is possible to detect a number of signs of shifts in attitude already occurring such as to suggest the process of adaptation might not be too traumatic, although it would need to be facilitated by less reactionary mass media than those currently dominant in much of the industrialised world. Likewise there would be a need for much more open and flexible education systems, with far less emphasis on the purpose of preparation for employment – or production of 'human capital'.

In place of the work ethic

It is, as already noted, a deeply ingrained value in most human societies that to undertake some form of work is the moral and social obligation of each individual. At the most basic level this is seen by most people as the essential way of establishing entitlement to a livelihood – despite which it is also accepted, in all but communistic societies where property rights are largely abolished, that ownership of assets (whether acquired or inherited) may entitle individuals to live without working. At the same time, beyond this sense of obligation, it has become commonplace – particularly in Western industrial societies of the modern era – to see work, in the sense of a more or less full-time occupation, as defining the identity of an individual.

Such a generally held value – which may be seen as a crucial prop to social solidarity – is not to be despised or lightly dismissed; it has in any case been so assiduously instilled and reinforced (as well as ruthlessly exploited) by different ruling elites over centuries that it may not be easily or quickly overturned. However, as we have observed, its underlying ideological assumptions are being challenged as never before by the impact of technological change and the effective limits to expansion of production and consumption on a finite planet. These pressures are already being reflected in changing attitudes, which seem likely to spread further and mutate in the face of evolving economic realities.

Thus, although there is a lack of survey data measuring trends over time, there is considerable anecdotal evidence suggesting that perceptions of work have changed quite radically in industrialised societies in recent years. This tendency is reflected in:

- *Dissolving ties to employers.* It has become a commonplace since the 1970s that the idea of a 'job for life' – so widespread in the earlier part of the twentieth century in the industrialised West (even more so in Japan) – is in the process of disappearing. This trend has been caused by a number of factors – notably (a) rapid technological change and the consequent incidence of higher productivity and reduced need for manpower for a given level of output, and (b) intensifying competition in the more globalised market combined with rising unemployment and the consequently dwindling bargaining power of labour. The result is a greater casualisation of workforces – with a rising proportion of workers on term contracts and enjoying reduced benefits. This in turn promotes a growing tendency, contrary to what is claimed by human resource management experts, for workers to be viewed as largely expendable commodities, who in their turn feel less and less commitment or loyalty to the organisations for which they work.

- *Spreading sense of pointlessness of work.* Along with the increasing commodification of workers there has, not surprisingly, developed a sense among many employees that they have little or no meaningful role in their jobs such as to give them a sense of their own identity or of a purpose other than that of simply turning up so as to collect a pay cheque at the end of the month.[1] By the same token there is a perception that employer organisations themselves are finding it increasingly hard to instil in their staff any sense that they have a meaningful role

---

1. See Richard Sennett, *The Culture of the New Capitalism* (New Haven: Yale University Press, 2006).

or motivation to work hard.[2] (Of course it would be wrong to suggest this description applies to all categories of worker – but perhaps more specifically to the very large number who are in menial, clerical or even middle-management positions, who are also those most liable to be made redundant when rationalisation is required.)

• *Abandonment of the idea of a career.* Faced with the reality that formal employment opportunities that are secure, fulfilling and financially rewarding are becoming ever more scarce, a growing number of younger people are looking at alternative lifestyles and activities. In Britain this is manifested in the apparent growth in volunteering, perhaps suggesting a perception that the prospect of having a career in the traditional sense is no longer either appealing or attainable for most of them. As against this, voluntary work may appear, particularly for young people, to offer (at least for relatively short periods) a more satisfying activity without necessarily entailing huge financial sacrifice – given that volunteers can still receive state welfare benefits.[3] It may also be the case that many people are attracted by the fact that as volunteers they are working for a non-profit organisation. Ironically perhaps, the whole process is being encouraged by government – at both national and local level (and by both main parties) – evidently because they perceive volunteers to be a potential source of cheap labour for the charities that are increasingly being used to deliver social services which it is perhaps felt the state can no longer afford to provide at market rates of pay.

• *Greater importance of creativity.* Another novel feature of the modern economy is that, while production of both goods and

2. See Maier, *Hello Laziness.*

3. See Libby Brooks, 'Ellie and Gordon Set a Good Example: Voluntary Service Trumps Compulsion', *Guardian*, 6 August 2009.

services is both less capital-intensive and less labour-intensive, it is more knowledge- or skills-intensive (albeit only for a small proportion of employees).[4] This is a function of a number of factors, including rapidly changing technology and the greater importance of services (including arts and entertainment) in the overall composition of consumer demand. In relation to the demand for manpower and the pattern of employment this trend means that it is often more cost-effective from the perspective of both employers and the individuals concerned (with the relevant skills or talent) for the latter to be hired on an ad hoc basis when needed rather than as permanent members of staff. As a result, a growing proportion of the workforce now tends to operate on a freelance basis, which also results in their being freer to take up other activities, whether paid or not. This tendency would evidently be reinforced by the establishment of a Citizen's Income assuring the basic means of survival. It would appropriately be further encouraged by official promotion – in conjunction with a more flexible educational curriculum – of creativity in the broadest sense, covering not merely the arts and sciences but sport and other recreational activities. In this way it might be possible to fulfil the dream of William Morris that 'one day we shall win back Art ... to our daily labour'.[5] Some of a more libertarian orientation would extend this idea even further by asserting that there should be no moral obligation to use free time to undertake any useful or improving activity, but rather that the true liberation permitted by the ending of 'wage slavery' should also be an opportunity to develop family and personal relationships.[6]

---

4. See Shutt, *The Trouble with Capitalism*, ch. 7.
5. *Art and Socialism* (1884).
6. Gorz, *Critique of Economic Reason.*

- *Acceptance of long-term worklessness.* Another facet of the revolution in the labour market is the seeming recognition in a
  number of developed countries that a large number of people
  have come to be perceived as unemployable in relation to the
  actual or potential demand for their limited skills. In Britain
  such people – accounting for as much as 9–10 per cent of the
  labour force – have come to be classified as effectively disabled
  and therefore eligible for incapacity benefit,[7] even though many
  of them would be quite willing and able to work if only there
  were effective demand – that is, at minimally adequate levels
  of pay – for their labour.

Such apparent trends in attitudes would seem to be in tune
with the idea that, in face of remorselessly growing imbalances
in the global labour market, working – in the sense of having
or seeking a job – should no longer be seen as an essential
precondition of the right to exist in human society, and that
alternatively (as proposed in Chapter 6) all should be entitled to
a basic income as of right. It remains true, however, that such a
notion is seen as inherently repugnant by a large number of people
who are not necessarily anxious to perpetuate the exploitation
of labour. It may therefore be appropriate, in order to counteract
the persistent cultural bias in favour of the obligation to work, to
seek an ideological justification for accepting that those who are
content to survive on a modest income, rather than compete for

---

7. Although the government has continually proclaimed its resolve to reduce
the numbers claiming this benefit, its persistent failure to do so betrays the reality
that it is also anxious to avoid the political embarrassment of having to reclassify
many of them as unemployed. As far as can be determined from available OECD
data, similar concerns relating to those members of the labour force classified as
disabled affect Canada, Denmark, France, Germany, the Netherlands, Norway,
Poland, Portugal, Sweden and Switzerland especially. See *Transforming Disability
into Ability* (Paris: OECD, 2003).

the positions which give access to greater material rewards, should be empowered by society to do so.

One of the more compelling justifications to have been advanced by advocates of the basic/citizen's income concept rests on the perception that the level of productivity within a given economy is to be viewed as both a collective and a cumulative phenomenon. This is because the ability of an individual worker – or proprietor of a business – to supply a given product or service depends on the collective capacity and insights of others within society, both living and dead, from which it follows that all may reasonably be entitled to a share in the product of this 'cognitive capital'.[8] In this sense those receiving basic income as a right of citizenship without necessarily doing any measurable work (other than what might be required of them as an emblematic contribution of, say, annual community service) could be considered as no more parasitic than those living off accumulated family wealth are at present.

Such a perspective is arguably akin to the notion of a 'global commons' – a term normally used to designate the elements of the biosphere (such as air, forests and water) which no individual or private entity can be deemed to own – but are to be utilised to the common benefit of all. As such it is clearly a diametric negation of the view that almost any economic asset can or should be transformed into private property with a view to yielding an exclusive profit for the owners.

While it is obviously hard to foresee what the dynamics of such a transformed labour market would turn out to be, it seems that access to a basic income could impact very favourably on those wishing to pursue creative or social/caring activities which may or may not yield an income – who, as suggested above, appear to

---

8. A. Fumagalli and S. Lucarelli, 'Basic Income and Productivity in Cognitive Capitalism', *Review of Social Economics*, January 2008.

be a growing minority of the labour force – in an atmosphere of relative freedom from financial pressure.

Changing perceptions of the corporate sector

As suggested in Chapter 3, there are grounds for believing that the dominance of big corporations – which may be seen as the institutional expression of generations of capital accumulation – may be coming under threat from smaller rivals which are not burdened with a huge inheritance of assets on which they are obliged to earn a profit. At the same time the pressures that such established corporations find themselves under to produce profits in line with the demands of the financial markets often lead them to pursue policies which are seen to conflict with the public interest – such as providing dangerous or overpriced products, failing to protect the environment or unduly exploiting labour in poor countries (not to mention their increasingly indifferent attitude to their staff generally – see above). While such adverse publicity has long been a significant irritant to the corporate sector, it is arguable that the cumulative weight of recent criticism has resulted in a more serious deterioration in their public image than in the past. This problem has unquestionably been exacerbated by the monumental excesses and irresponsibility of the banking sector that have come to light since 2007, coming as they do hard on the heels of the huge and criminal bankruptcies of Enron and WorldCom exposed in 2001–02 following the dotcom collapse.

Perhaps a still more serious threat to the survival of traditional corporations as independent entities is the manifest failure of the established mechanisms of corporate governance to curb their excesses. One of the perennial weaknesses of the joint-stock (shareholder) company model is the so-called agency problem: the difficulty faced by shareholders in ensuring that the company's managers run it in their interests (as the owners). This was the reason why Adam Smith considered the joint-stock model a bad one,[9] despite which its proliferation in Britain was encouraged by the Companies Acts of the 1850s (see Chapter 6), which crucially offered them the automatic right to limited liability. For all the subsequent efforts to strengthen corporate governance by shareholders it has proved difficult if not impossible to prevent abuses by management. A spectacular example of this was the vote by shareholders of Royal Dutch Shell in May 2009 to deny bonuses awarded by the board to the top management in spite of their failure to meet predetermined performance targets. The brazen refusal of the board to accept the results of this vote as binding – as it was legally entitled to do – was a blatant demonstration that corporate management is effectively beyond the control of companies' owners, let alone of the wider community.

Another source of deepening popular disenchantment with the corporate sector, which is arguably the source of its greatest vulnerability, is its ever growing dependence on state subsidies. For if it is perceived that private-sector companies cannot survive without such support, it is not hard to see that belief in the beneficence of the profit motive may be permanently undermined in so far as

1. the corporate sector's inability to generate adequate returns on capital without public subsidy will cast doubt on the viability of the profit-maximising model of enterprise;

2. the moral hazard stemming from the implicit taxpayer guarantee of private companies, with all the associated scope for conflicts of interest, corruption and waste, will inspire terminal revulsion on the part of the public – if it has not already become financially unsustainable.

---

9. *The Wealth of Nations*, Book 5.

Just as the cumulative effect of such flaws in the functioning of the existing system is making the public more and more disillusioned with corporations fatally dependent on their need to maximise profits for shareholders, they may be increasingly drawn to forms of enterprise that do not need to generate profits – or are even precluded by their statutes from doing so. Often these will be state-owned companies, as when they are effectively inheritors of a large failed private-sector company that has to be taken into public ownership by default in order to avoid serious market disruption. To a growing extent, however, there are signs of a propensity to favour models of enterprise which are much smaller in scale and tend to be perceived as less remote and more in tune with the concerns and aspirations of the wider community. (Moreover, as noted earlier, smaller companies are also likely to grow in importance in so far as there is less and less need for new market entrants to have large quantities of capital.) Examples of this tendency include:

• *Microfinance and micro-enterprises.* This concept has its origin in Bangladesh, one of the world's poorest countries, where it was conceived as a mechanism for enabling individuals (mainly women) without assets or skills to start small businesses (such as egg production and marketing) using small unsecured loans – the kind of lending that is not economical for a commercial bank to support.[10] In various forms this model has been replicated all over the world and has inspired the creation since the early 1990s of what are known as community development finance institutions in the USA and Britain (with some government support), supporting existing as well as new small businesses not catered for by commercial banks.

---

10. The concept was the brainchild of Muhammad Yunus, founder of Grameen Bank, who was subsequently awarded the Nobel Peace Prize.

- *Community companies and enterprises.* Various mechanisms have been developed in Britain in recent years for enabling local communities to establish companies with a view to creating or taking over existing businesses – such as shops, public houses or petrol stations – which may not be viable on the basis of a traditional capitalist model but which may be able to survive on a non-profit basis. Ownership may be on a mutual or cooperative basis. In Germany the longer established, municipally owned *Stadtwerke* fulfil a comparable function (albeit on a larger scale of operation) in respect of energy and water utilities in many cities.

- *Informal interest groups.* Groups wishing to exchange ideas and provide services, of which the Linux movement (see Chapter 3) is perhaps the best-known example, often apparently prefer to provide services on a non-profit basis.

While it is difficult to draw definitive conclusions based on the emergence of such trends, they do appear to be consistent with the hypothesis that the human species is tending to evolve beyond the type of *Homo economicus* (motivated primarily if not exclusively by self-seeking) in which the classical economists tended to cast it. If so, it may be hoped that this change reflects a perception that the competitive instincts viewed so positively by Adam Smith, Ricardo and their latter-day heirs are increasingly inappropriate in an ever more complex and overcrowded world, where our survival will depend much more on our capacity to cooperate with each other.

Marginalising the profit motive

It would of course be extremely naive and unrealistic to suggest that the propensity of human beings to be self-seeking is in the process of dying out. Hence defenders of the profits system are justified in pointing out that the greed which is ritually identified as the root of the financial and economic crisis is an inescapable fact of life. On the other hand it must also be recognised that the present structures of standard company law effectively define the pursuit of profit maximisation as a public good. That is because companies are legally the property of their shareholders, in whose interests they are to be managed. While that does not necessarily require the management to pursue the maximisation of profit (whether in the short or the long term) under all circumstances, a brief consideration of corporate dynamics suggests this is almost always going to be the overriding consideration in that

- given a large number of shareholders in a typical company (who cannot all be consulted on any particular decision), it is not possible for the management (board of directors) to assume any priority other than those consistent with profit maximisation – the lowest common denominator – in reaching policy decisions;
- in a competitive market it is reasonable for the management to assume that their own interests and those of the shareholders (most of whom are investing for income) are best served by a policy that will produce the highest return on their investment, bearing in mind that if they fail to deliver such returns the share price will fall, the company may be taken over and they as managers are likely to lose their jobs.

In view of this stark reality it is in order to treat any suggestion from chief executives that they will give equal weight to the concerns of other 'stakeholders' (such as workers and consumers) – not to mention the lavish publicity campaigns of energy companies seeking to suggest that the preservation of the environment is central to their business model and the core of their 'mission statement' – with enormous cynicism.

If this analysis is valid it follows that the reason for the continuing primacy of the profit motive in the economy is to be found in the central principles of company law. Hence if the profit motive is to be subordinated to other concerns it must also follow that company law will either need to be modified or effectively bypassed. In fact, it should be clear that restrictions on the independence of companies that are operating in areas of public concern and with effective public support or protection – as outlined in the last chapter – would have the effect of marginalising shareholder interests.

If such an approach were adopted, therefore, it would mean that, while the profit motive would not be abolished (an impossibility), it would no longer be elevated to the level of a public virtue. In other words private greed would no longer be effectively incentivised or mandated by law. Moreover, such an orientation would, as already suggested, both remove the distorting influence of the profit motive on the determination of economic priorities and permit the release of a large share of economic value-added for more useful purposes (see Chapter 6).

Measuring welfare

As already made clear, the traditional calculus of GDP will need to be retained, at least for the foreseeable future, as the essential indicator of a country's financial welfare and therefore the size of the potential tax base. What should no longer be acceptable, however, is that it should be regarded as an indicator of economic or social welfare. This is partly because it manifestly fails to capture economic activity based on unpaid labour, such as that of family carers, which nonetheless adds substantial economic value. The significance of this gap in the computation of economic value-added seems likely, moreover, to increase as the amount of voluntary work rises in both absolute and relative terms. Another serious deficiency of GDP as a true measure of welfare is that, since it is simply an aggregation of all paid transactions in the economy, it takes no account of the net impact on human welfare. Thus, for example, the value of the production and consumption of tobacco is added to that of the resources devoted to remedying the resulting damage to health, whereas a more rational computation of welfare would suggest that the latter should be netted from the former.

However, the complexity of any attempt to recalculate GDP to take account of such anomalies would evidently be so great as to preclude undertaking such an exercise so as to forge a single new indicator of aggregate value-added more closely reflecting true economic welfare. Equally a measure of the well-being of a national (or any other) community based on a simple average of any aggregate of value-added – even a more accurate and comprehensive one than traditional GDP – fails to reflect the distribution of income. For, as is increasingly recognised, based on the evidence of comparative sociological surveys, relative income equality is positively correlated with indicators of social well-being – such as high life expectancy and low incidence of mental illness.[11] Thus each national community seriously seeking to enhance its collective welfare will need to formulate a set of criteria and indicators that are deemed to reflect this and then devise appropriate policies and strategies accordingly.

---

11. Kate Pickett and Richard Wilkinson, *The Spirit Level: Why Greater Equality Makes Societies Stronger* (London: Bloomsbury, 2009).

8

Deepening democracy

IT IS PERHAPS scarcely necessary to point out that the radically different type of economy and society described in the last three chapters presupposes a political system that is just as radically transformed compared with the ones presently prevailing either in the industrialised West or anywhere else. The reason for this is that the kind of drastic changes in economic orientation that are proposed would be completely at variance with the agenda of the currently dominant vested interests – representing big business in general and big finance in particular – so that there is no chance of achieving or sustaining such changes unless and until the latter's influence has been effectively neutralised. In short, what is needed is a political order that is far more genuinely democratic and capable of reflecting the popular will than the present structures – or indeed anything that has gone before.

But while this may be obvious to many, it is far from being accepted by the official myth-makers and propagandists of the industrialised Western countries who represent the heart of the global establishment. For, according to their well-worn slogans, these nations exemplify the principles of democracy, individual liberty and the rule of law which they are continually urging the rest of the world to apply – and which are indeed enshrined in the Universal Declaration of Human Rights adopted in 1948. Yet quite apart from the more obvious hypocrisies manifest in such claims (such as Western support for favoured dictators and launching of wars in breach of the UN charter) it is increasingly difficult for them to maintain that simply by holding periodic elections of legislators and other public officials under universal suffrage they are assuring anything that can be described as genuinely representative government – even assuming that the integrity of the ballot can also be assured (something that may no longer be taken for granted since the US presidential election of 2000).

Ending the power of money over the political process

Despite this official complacency it is widely perceived that the present system of political funding in the industrialised world (and, even more so, in the developing world) is neither equitable nor transparent, and that in consequence it seriously distorts the political process. This is because of the lack of any effective restraint on the ability of moneyed interests to make financial contributions to politicians and parties and thereby influence their electoral platforms and the policies they pursue once in office. As a result it is undeniable that 'big finance' is the dominant influence over the political agenda in many countries (particularly the United States) – to the point where, as is claimed by some, the USA has come to resemble a one-party state, given that both major parties are subverted by this corruption in equal measure to broadly the same effect. To a large extent, it may be added, Britain has begun to follow the same pattern – in thrall to the same vested interests – since the 1980s, even if the sums of money involved are trivial compared with the billions of dollars now spent on the US political process. It is true that different specific favours are sought and obtained by different commercial interests from different parties, but the interest groups concerned mostly tend to have a common belief in the desirability of minimal regulation of business and low taxation.

Nowhere has their venial power been more disastrously demonstrated than by the Wall Street lobby's success since the 1980s in securing the removal of all the restraints which had been imposed on the financial sector during the 1930s (see Chapter 1). Just as conspicuously anti-democratic has been the massive deployment of lobbying and campaigning resources by the healthcare and 'big pharma' lobby in the USA in 2009 with the overt intention of subverting the clear electoral mandate given to President Obama and the Democrats in Congress in favour of major reform of the healthcare sector, including greater involvement of the public sector.

Thus it can reasonably be argued that the electoral process in the USA – and likewise in Britain and other Western 'democracies' – is no better designed to reflect the popular will or public interest than it was before the introduction of universal suffrage in the late nineteenth or early twentieth centuries, when the power of moneyed interests to influence the political process was more explicitly built into the constitution (with the franchise based on a property qualification) than it is today. The required remedies, which have been well known for many years to all seriously interested parties (who regrettably do not include the vast majority of the public), are essentially the following.

Political funding

Legally constituted political parties (defined as those with a certified membership above a certain threshold) should only be allowed to receive financial contributions from individual members – at a single flat rate – to which funding from the state would be added in proportion to the total sum raised from members. The aim of such a provision, it should be clear, would be to incentivise parties to develop a mass membership to which the leadership would have to remain responsive rather than be able to ignore them in favour of accepting financial support from outside – as notoriously has happened with Britain's Labour Party, which in the ten years following its return to power in 1997 saw its membership fall from 405,000 to 177,000 (reportedly the lowest level in its hundred-year history).[1]

Separate regulations would need to be devised so as to limit the power of unrepresentative moneyed interests to fund propaganda relating to referenda or other single-issue campaigns (e.g. in support of or opposition to specific legislation such as the current proposed reform of the US healthcare sector referred to above). These could take the form of an effective ban on the contributing of funds or other material support to any campaign or body external to itself by any corporate organisation enjoying the privileges of limited liability or other public subsidy or protection. Assuming that under reformed corporate legislation (as proposed in Chapter 6) most companies not benefiting from such privileges would probably be small firms with limited financial resources available to spend on campaigning or lobbying, these restrictions should have the effect of marginalising the impact of big money in relation to political campaigns conducted outside the normal electoral process.

Limit on patronage

Public officials, whether elected or appointed, should be barred from accepting or holding

---

1. 'Labour Party Membership Falls to Lowest Level since it was Founded in 1900', *Daily Telegraph*, 30 July 2008.

- any form of emolument (including 'consultancy' fees) other than their official salaries – which should be set at sufficient levels to discourage corruption – while they are in office;
- paid employment with corporations or interest groups of any kind for several years after they leave office, in return for which they would be assured an adequate official pension.[2]

It is not appropriate here to address all the well-worn but spurious arguments against such reforms – such as that the public do not want their taxes spent on supporting political parties, or that restrictions on the receipt of patronage will discourage many of the best candidates from entering public life. For ultimately the conclusion must be that any less restrictive reforms will leave in place an open invitation to corruption of public officials and subversion of the political process.

Limiting media distortions

It goes without saying that a genuinely democratic system of government requires that the public have both maximum access to factual information and exposure to opinion-forming mass media which reflect as broad a range of views as possible. Hence the ability of a small number of individuals or corporations – representing a very narrow range of sectional interests – to exercise effective editorial control over significant parts of the media is incompatible with ensuring that the media are both broadly representative of a cross-section of opinion as well as open to the expression of new ideas. Moreover, this status quo is all the more unacceptable in so far as newspaper proprietors, as is almost invariably the case, turn out to share the agenda of big business – or, to the extent that they do not, they may be induced to amend their editorial policy

---

2. Shutt, *A New Democracy*, ch. 6.

in response to more or less covert pressure from major advertisers on whom they are significantly dependent for revenue.

It follows that the power of individual media magnates – or indeed of any private-sector corporation accountable only to its shareholders – to exercise this kind of dominance over major newspapers or broadcast media channels will need to be eliminated. Under the kind of reformed structure of company law outlined in Chapter 6 this could in theory be achieved quite easily – by withdrawing the right of such media companies to limited liability status, except on condition that they gave some meaningful commitment to genuine openness and balance in both reporting and comment (under the aegis of a publicly accountable supervisory body of some kind). In that event it is more than likely that most existing proprietors would abandon the business rather than surrender autonomous editorial control, since most mass-circulation newspapers have become progressively more unprofitable over the decades since the advent of television, so that the only attraction of continued ownership is the political power that comes with it (contrary to what most proprietors publicly proclaim).

In fact, bearing in mind the current dramatic developments in the media – centred mainly on the Internet – it is quite possible that the pattern of access to news and views relating to the most burning issues of public policy will follow such a radically transformed pattern that it may seem neither possible nor necessary to regulate it. This is because, as noted in Chapter 3, largely free access to the Internet (for both users and providers of material) is causing the business models of the traditional media to disintegrate – as they are less and less able to compete with innovative start-up media companies for whom market entry costs are now negligible – except perhaps in the case of those organisations which are in receipt of state subsidies, such as the BBC. It is thus conceivable that the flow of information and opinions will be so profuse and fragmented that both media moguls and governments will find it more difficult than at present to manipulate opinion through the media (short of overt censorship, which it is hard to imagine being accepted in Western democracies, as flawed as they may be).

Yet even if the advent of new media via the Internet is undermining the existing model of big-business dominance of the media, there is little cause for complacency. For given the ruthless determination of organised corporate interests to maintain their effective monopoly of power, it is certain that they will fight by all means at their disposal to combat what they see as subversive forces. Even if they fail, however, this will leave crucial question-marks over the future shape of the media – such as what kind of organisations will take responsibility for assuring adequately broad and reasonably reliable news coverage and how they will be financed – for which there is no obvious answer, particularly bearing in mind that it is not possible to eliminate bias through the selectiveness of reporting. It may well be that some element of public subsidy will prove to be part of the answer in any event.

What needs to be accepted, however, is that there can be no foolproof way of assuring totally unbiased, 'value-free' reporting – let alone unbiased comment or analysis – because of the inevitable selectiveness of the process of gathering and reporting of the 'facts'.[3] The best hope may therefore be that the diversity of sources of information now developing on the Internet, many of them operating without the support or distorting influence of advertisers, will be so great as to prevent the 'corporate media' or any other single vested interest from creating a monolithic uniformity of public perceptions of truth in defiance of objective reality.

---

3. See D. Cromwell and D. Edwards, *Newspeak in the 21st Century* (London: Pluto Press, 2009).

Restoring the rule of law

Important as the reform of the institutions of democratic representation and accountability undoubtedly is, it can count for very little if the rule of law is not effectively upheld. For if, as is now more and more manifestly the case in the supposed democracies of the industrialised West, those who are responsible for enforcing the law fail to discharge that duty – while at the same time ordinary citizens are effectively prevented from holding them to account, not least by the prohibitive cost of litigation – then in practice 'democracy' is little different from tyranny. Of the innumerable instances of such failure in recent years that could be cited, the following (drawn mainly from US and British experience) serve to illustrate the extent of the malady:

1. the failure to initiate any meaningful prosecutions for war crimes, torture or other abuses committed by US and British officials in connection with the 'war on terror' declared in 2001 or the invasion of Iraq in 2003 (this while various leaders of smaller powers have been indicted for such crimes before the recently established International Criminal Court or other tribunals set up at the Hague or elsewhere);
2. failure to prosecute cases of criminal fraud – including mortgage fraud – even where there was ample evidence to support such action (some in the public domain) – as in the case of the subsequently convicted fraudster Bernard Madoff, against whom many warnings were given to the Securities and Exchange Commission several years before he was finally brought to justice in 2009;
3. the decision not to pursue allegations of corruption against BAE Systems (over arms deals with Saudi Arabia) in response to pressure from the Saudi authorities;

4. failure to prosecute cases of illegal invasion of privacy by British tabloid newspapers.

The most disturbing aspect of this systematic laxity is that it tends to exacerbate rather than diminish a global climate of spreading lawlessness. For whereas until quite recently atrocities such as the Tienanmen massacre in Beijing of 1989 could be unequivocally condemned in the West without necessarily provoking charges of hypocrisy, there is now a sense that the authorities in most countries are willingly embracing a moral position which readily accepts the use of reasons of state – or simple corruption – to condone apparently criminal acts. Whether or not this is symptomatic of a wilful attempt on the part of the elite to promote a climate of permissiveness towards misdeeds of the rich and powerful, it bodes ill for any attempt to restore and extend respect for the rule of law, which will be vital to the creation of any international order to be based on agreed principles and goals.

Enhancing participation and accountability

Aside from the need to improve the transparency and equity of the process of democratic representation and the ways in which information and opinions are disseminated and influenced, there is a widespread feeling in the industrialised world that ordinary citizens need to gain more influence over the content of government than is afforded them by the periodic marking of ballot papers. The approaches that societies have adopted – or may try to adopt – in order thus to 'empower' individual citizens or groups is a vast subject, to which it is not possible to do adequate justice in the present context and on which it is therefore only possible to reach very general conclusions. Such caution is in any case dictated by the view enunciated earlier that the only durable form of such institutional change will be evolutionary rather than revolutionary. Nevertheless, given the importance of this issue for determining the nature and functioning of a post-capitalist, decommodified era the world now needs to enter, it is appropriate to point out the potentially most significant broad areas of innovation. These may be seen as

1. greater power of citizens to hold elected officials to account in relation to both their personal integrity and their political commitments;
2. the enhanced right of citizens to initiate both legislative and policy change through petitions and referenda – that is, without necessarily having to persuade their elected representatives to take action on their behalf;
3. the devolution of the maximum power to regional or local level (consistent with acceptable levels of efficiency in resource use) so as to enhance citizens' and communities' power to control their own lives, particularly in relation to economic activity – however, such devolution to local communities must not occur at the expense of other communities or to the detriment of greater global harmonisation, cooperation and integration, which will be more than ever indispensable to survival in a crowded and fragile planet.

Clearly the possibility of thus giving citizens greater control over their own lives has been greatly advanced by developments in modern telecommunications and the electronic media. Just as significant in enhancing their autonomy, however, is the change in lifestyles arising from the progressive diminution in the importance of paid employment or self-employment in people's more extended lives – see Chapter 7. For one activity that people would readily find more time for in the absence of productive work opportunities would surely be what might be termed 'active citizenship'. Thus potentially the human race could rediscover the opportunity to practice direct democracy somewhat in the manner of the ancient Athenians – but without their need to depend on slaves to do all the menial work.

The measure of democracy

It may by now be scarcely a matter of dispute that drastic reform of the functioning of our supposedly democratic institutions is urgently needed. However, one perhaps does not need to be unduly cynical to reflect (based on even a cursory reading of history) that human institutions are by their nature imperfect and fallible and that any structures are to some extent liable to be subverted through one source of corruption or another. Hence while in theory reforms to the political process along the lines outlined above should logically result in government that is more equitable and representative of popular aspirations than is the case under the existing regime, such an outcome cannot be guaranteed.

It will therefore be vital for the public to be able to demand and receive information on economic, social and other indicators – such as those referred to in Chapter 7 – which should properly be seen as a reflection of how far democracy could be deemed to exist other than as an institutional abstraction. For if it can be shown, for example, that income or wealth distribution in a given community remains significantly skewed – such that the richest 30 per cent of the population has an average income of more than, say, five times that of the remaining 70 per cent – it would be legitimate to query how far this could be considered the plausible outcome of a truly democratic political process. Hence it will be important to reinforce institutional enhancements to the democratic process along the lines outlined above by fostering an ideology of greater social solidarity and equality – in strong contrast to that of self-centred individualism so strongly promoted during the neoliberal era of the last thirty years.

Governance in the developing world

In principle there is no reason why the approach outlined above for bringing about more genuine accountability in supposed 'democracies' should not be seen as applicable to all countries. However, it is important to recognise that the model of governance implied by it is that of a state which is not only legally sovereign but able to conduct its affairs on a substantially independent basis. Yet in reality such a description does not fit a large number of the world's smallest and poorest countries, which are nominally independent but nonetheless dependent for their survival on flows of external aid – and in the case of several of the smallest (typically island states in the Caribbean, the Pacific and elsewhere) are likely to remain so permanently.

The difficulty that would arise in such cases is that there is a disjuncture in accountability resulting from the fact that the source of the external aid is different from that of the government's locally generated revenue. Hence in practice – as many who have been responsible for supervising aid programmes can attest – there is a tendency for this divided responsibility to create confusion over whether Third World governments can and should be more answerable to foreign donors in the stewardship of aid funds than to their own people who are supposed to be the beneficiaries of them. The net result under present aid programme practice is often, not surprisingly, a failure to utilise the aid responsibly from the perspective of either party and a loss of any effective accountability. This has been the cause of justified criticism of aid programmes – for which there is nevertheless no substitute, at least for the foreseeable future.

The problems raised by aid dependency and the largely unsuccessful attempts to resolve them over several decades is a topic too complex to be addressed in detail here. Yet few would probably dissent from the conclusion that a major reason (but not the only one) for the failure of aid programmes has been the extreme ambivalence of donors over the whole question of development – and their compulsive tendency to use their programmes to achieve their own national foreign policy or commercial ends (notably during the Cold War), applying conditionality which all too often amounts to a negation of development (e.g. financial liberalisation). Such problems are too often compounded by conflicts among bilateral donors that commonly arise from their competitive pursuit of narrow national interests – at the expense of those of the supposed beneficiaries. The legacy of this historic approach, which still persists in spite of greater public awareness of the increasingly desperate plight of most developing countries, is a tainted relationship based on corruption and mutual suspicion that has reinforced the abusive tendencies of many developing-country governments. For these often merely pay lip-service to the idea of poverty reduction in order to get their hands on donor funds – often with a view to reinforcing their own quasi-feudal regimes. They are also prone, it should be noted, to take an equally irresponsible attitude to borrowing money on commercial terms from abroad (whether from governments or private lenders), where the lenders are often able effectively to bribe developing-country leaders to accept loans which offer little or no benefit to the country but impose an unaffordable debt burden on their impoverished people.

Given such a legacy, it will be vital to try to recast completely the relationship between donor and recipient states on a basis that could be more likely to encourage the latter to assume their responsibilities, free of the 'moral hazard' associated with implicit guarantees of donor support. There would seem to be two possible alternative approaches to achieving this goal, both highly problematic.

1. For states meeting minimum basic criteria of democratically accountable governance, there would be annual lump-sum transfers of aid from the international community – via a single UN agency – to the government budget. This amount, which would be determined as a function of population size and GDP per head, would be on unconditional terms – except that a fixed percentage should be allocated for distribution in the form of a basic income transfer to all adults. The rest would be allocated at the government's discretion for which it would be answerable only to its own people. No additional donor funds would be receivable except in case of a natural disaster. In the event that (a) donor or loans funds were accepted by it from any other external source (public or private)[4] or (b) democratic accountability were deemed to have been suspended, a beneficiary country would lose its entitlement to multilateral (UN) funds. The annual transfer entitlement would be subject to periodic review and renewal (say every five years), with a sliding scale of incentive bonuses/penalties applicable in order to encourage increased internal tax raising – especially of direct taxes. (While one could readily envisage difficulties with the administration of such a system, the effort of overcoming them would prove worthwhile if (a) it led to developing countries achieving greater economic self-reliance to match their supposed political independence, and (b) it

---

4. Other than for needed investment in commercial projects (e.g. mineral development) that could not be foreseen within the public investment programme. Such exceptional funding from abroad (including any sovereign loans) would need to be approved by the UN donor agency against strict criteria guaranteeing that any resulting debt-service payments would be generated exclusively from the project itself.

were thereby possible to convince sceptical opinion in the donor countries that aid to the recipients was to some extent conditional on their willingness to help themselves). States failing to meet these basic criteria would be entitled to receive only limited humanitarian aid.

2. Sovereignty would be surrendered to or combined with other states or groups of states (ideally on a regional basis), which would comprise a sufficiently large tax-revenue base to support the poorer and more vulnerable territories. The latter's relationship with the centre would thus become analogous to that of peripheral parts of European or other developed countries (e.g. the Scottish islands or Sicily) which benefit from indefinite explicit or implicit support grants from the centre, on which they are thus deemed to be permanently dependent. Under such an arrangement the territories concerned would then be part of a larger political entity in which its democratic representation would be on a par (that is, proportionate to its size) with all other parts of the union. The accountability problem associated with aid programmes – and the related problems of corruption – would thus be avoided.[5]

Although the presumption is that all countries – or groupings of countries – should be free to pursue their autonomously determined economic strategies, it is to be stressed that this would be in a global climate of far greater official intervention and regulation of market forces – and corresponding rejection of the liberalisation favoured by the Washington Consensus – than has prevailed since the 1980s (see Chapter 6). Rather there should be a new global

---

5. While the obstacles to forming such regional groupings may seem formidable – particularly in the light of the chronic ineffectiveness of such organisations as the Association of Southeast Asian Nations (ASEAN) – there have recently been signs that the need for them is being more widely recognised (see Chapter 6).

consensus based on the twin pillars of (a) cooperation rather than competition and (b) national or regional economic autonomy.

It will be immediately apparent that such a radical restructuring of the relationship between developed and developing countries is far removed from what is likely to be seen as politically acceptable by any of the major parties involved under present circumstances. Indeed at a time when many new 'donor' countries such as China and the oil-rich Gulf states appear as determined to exploit poor but resource-rich countries in Africa and elsewhere as the Western imperial powers ever were in the past – almost regardless of the consequences for the local population – any advocacy of such a new approach might well be dismissed as pure fantasy. This is all the more likely given the obvious complexities involved in establishing such a new model on a workable basis. It may be noted, however, that such ideas are not out of line with the proposal of the distinguished Brandt Commission – put forward as long ago as 1980 (before the Washington Consensus had been invented) – that aid funds should be distributed on a 'universal and automatic' basis.[6] It has, moreover, to be faced that the combination of the manifestly failed and corrupting development aid model still in place and chronic global financial crisis has left the developing world at a point where it is more than ever a threat to world peace and stability – as failed states, civil disorder and forced migration proliferate across the globe.

6. *North–South: A Programme for Survival* (London: Pan, 1980).

9

Capitulation or catastrophe?

I N TRYING TO define the essential elements of a more rational type of economy and society for the future we have identified a number of tendencies that are already manifest – in response to developments such as the collapse of traditional labour markets and of business models rendered unsustainable by technological change and financial anarchy – which appear to be consistent with the more profound transformation being proposed. This might suggest that it is possible to achieve the kind of radical change that is needed through a relatively painless evolutionary process over time. Unfortunately, however, time is not necessarily on our side in the face of the major threats to our survival now looming. Of these none is more menacing than the monolithic power of a ruthlessly irresponsible global establishment seemingly determined to suppress the truth about the terminal failure of the existing order, or more depressing than the absence of organised opposition,[1]

---

1. The only significant source of dissent within the realm of formal political activity is that which has emerged in several Latin American countries since the late 1990s, starting in Venezuela under President Hugo Chávez.

at least in the industrialised world, outside the ranks of fringe terrorist groups.

A glimmer of hope?

Superficially, it could appear that the prospect of any weakening of the corrupt power of big business is as remote as ever in the wake of the 2007 credit crunch. Thus the ability of Wall Street in 2008 – through the mediation of its principal emissary to the administration of President George W. Bush, treasury secretary Henry Paulson – to procure trillions of dollars of public money in order, in effect, to pay off gambling debts of criminally reckless Wall Street speculators, with minimal resistance from Congress, suggests that the political dominance of big money is now as total as it is shameless. Similar breathtaking demonstrations of the overweening power of the financial community have been seen in Britain, where private-sector banks which have had to be partly or wholly nationalised – at a cost of hundreds of billions of pounds to the taxpayer – have been allowed to award their new senior executives million-pound packages of salary and bonuses without any apparent check to a repetition of the abuses that caused their downfall. Indeed governments on both sides of the Atlantic have been at pains to insist that they do not think they should be in the business of trying to influence the management of banks (even when they have become their reluctant owners) and should deal with their new acquisitions on an 'arms-length' basis. All the while both senior private-sector and public officials who are manifestly guilty of criminal negligence or outright fraud are not only not being prosecuted but are either allowed to keep their jobs or, if dismissed, given exorbitant 'golden handshakes'.

This blatant refusal by both governments and the financial sector to accept their responsibilities vis-à-vis the public interest

is of course profoundly dispiriting to any concerned citizen struggling to retain a belief that democratic accountability and the rule
of law are not just empty slogans. Yet when on top of such betray-
als it is suggested by the media that the huge addition to the fiscal
deficit and public debt resulting from this high-level private and
public profligacy will have to be paid for by its innocent victims,
ordinary citizens and taxpayers – through cuts in pensions and
other social welfare benefits (always preferred to tax rises by the
news managers[2]) – dismay starts turning to incredulity. Almost as
incredible is the alternative strategy – openly proposed by many
leading economists[3] – that the authorities should seek deliberately
to generate high rates of inflation by indefinitely sustaining an
expansionist monetary policy while holding down interest rates,
thereby progressively devaluing the massive debts in both private
and public sectors. For its advocates know all too well that such
a 'solution' to the debt problem can only succeed at the expense
of the vulnerable majority who are not debtors but live on small,
relatively fixed incomes or their modest savings, which stand
to be substantially wiped out by this process (as happened so
disastrously in the newly dissolved Soviet Union in 1992 as a result
of Western-inspired 'shock therapy').

At the time of writing, it is hard to tell whether such brazenly
inequitable and confiscatory proposals – which may be seen as the
culmination of thirty years of efforts to externalise the costs of
private-sector failure to the public at large – are likely to prove
more than just talk. However, if a serious attempt is made to
implement either or both of these strategies it may well appear,

---

2. A Google search of the supposedly impartial BBC *Newsnight*'s extensive
coverage in the April–June 2009 period of how to reduce the massive British public
deficit identifies four programmes dealing with spending cuts (24 April, 27 April, 4
June and 10 June), none mentioning tax increases.

3. See Professor Kenneth Rogoff, 'Embracing Inflation', *Guardian*, 2 December
2008.

paradoxically, to be grounds for a perverse kind of hope. For it is quite conceivable that such manifestly unjust and divisive policies will prove a catalyst for social unrest and more direct expressions of political opposition (violent or non-violent) than have been seen hitherto, in the industrialised world at least. At the same time the inevitable slide into a vicious circle of deepening deprivation and economic decline must, it might be supposed, force more people within the leadership to recognise that such socially regressive strategies cannot ultimately 'work' in terms of restoring economic and social equilibrium – and hence will also preclude any sustained recovery in the securities markets. In that event it is all too believable that the ultimate power brokers (those standing behind the visible public leadership) have contingency plans for a more comprehensive campaign of repression. On the other hand their ability to sustain this with the resources of an ever more fiscally bankrupt state may turn out to be limited, especially as deepening economic collapse and spreading disorder cause the far more deprived developing world to spin further out of control – for which the current inability of NATO forces to restore any kind of order to Afghanistan through their increasingly unaffordable military campaign seems likely to prove the paradigm.

At various points on this seemingly inevitable downward spiral – which may, somewhat arbitrarily, be dated from the bursting of the dotcom bubble and related financial scandals at the beginning of the century – the world's de facto rulers will continually be confronted with a decision about whether it is possible to sustain the delusion that the capitalist status quo can be preserved until, as if by some quasi-mystical process, recovery occurs and the next upswing of the business cycle begins. On this interpretation of the ruling elite's long-term strategy (if they have one at all) the point may come at which some of the leadership, having recognised that their own prospects (or that of the world as a whole) have become so dire that the status quo must be sacrificed, decide to break ranks and seek a more radical alternative.

It is thus possible to speculate that the world may be close to a point where space will at last be allowed for radically new visions of how the global economy could be reordered so as to prevent disasters such as the present crisis from recurring and to set it on a more sustainable path to the benefit of the vast majority. Equally, however, it seems likely that the catalyst for such a shift towards a more radical agenda is likely to be a traumatic event such as an even more profound financial upheaval than that of 2007–08.

An emergency response

In such circumstances, it is self-evident that the transition to a more rational, collectivist economic and social model along the lines delineated in the preceding chapters would not be achievable overnight. However, in order to avert the most dire consequences of the ongoing collapse of the existing model it will be essential to adopt certain radical measures without delay.

- *Restriction of cross-border capital flows.* As explained in Chapter 6, moves to reintroduce exchange controls and thus limit the convertibility of currencies – a regime which applied to a varying extent to all but the US dollar until around 1980 – would be the essential prerequisite to undoing the most harmful consequences of globalisation and restoring the ability of national or regional communities to exercise a degree of genuine autonomy. Yet in the crisis conditions of looming economic collapse such restrictions will be vital to (a) maintaining or restoring a minimum level of economic stability and (b) facilitating income redistribution by preventing capital flight.

- *Introduction of a flat-rate citizen's income* for all adults with residence qualification in a given country. Although this is seen as a long-term objective (see Chapter 6), its early introduction, on a transitional basis, would have immediate macroeconomic benefits in offsetting the effects of the rapid rise in job losses, house repossessions and other consequences of the slump in cutting real personal income levels sharply. In this regard it would be far more cost-effective than public works programmes (designed to generate employment) and/or tax breaks, which will have only limited offsetting impact given the likelihood that the relatively small number of beneficiaries will tend to use some of the proceeds to pay off debt rather than boost spending. In contrast it is likely that a basic Citizen's Income in the pocket of every adult would be nearly all spent on consumption, thus having a much greater 'multiplier' effect and thereby making a far greater contribution to stabilising the level of overall economic activity.

- *Transfer to full public ownership or mutual (non-profit) ownership of all deposit-taking financial institutions* (with public guarantees of all retail deposits). The same new non-profit institutions would assume responsibility for administering commercial loans – supporting production, fixed investment and trade – according to normal prudential criteria (but taking account of the need for short-term roll-over or refinancing where this might be justified to preserve activity during the exceptional conditions caused by the slump). However, their speculative bad loans and other assets would need to be liquidated or written off, in the first instance at the expense of existing shareholders and bondholders.

- Official intervention to *regulate and stabilise international trade flows and commodity markets* with a view to minimising the disruptive impact of the global recession (particularly for the benefit of the poorest countries and regions). This would entail (a) suspension of WTO rules so as to enable existing bilateral trade flows to be maintained in the short term without undue disruption by sudden influxes of low-cost products from third countries; and (b) moves to limit fluctuations in the prices of key commodities (notably food and energy) between a temporarily fixed floor and ceiling in each case (at the same time international agencies such as the World Food Programme would be enabled to acquire and make available adequate supplies to meet the needs of the poorest people in the poorest countries).

• *Increases in direct taxes* on both income and wealth of both companies and higher-earning individuals. Apart from consideration of the urgent need to close ballooning fiscal deficits this would be justified on the grounds that, given the diminished opportunities (reflecting the limited need) for new investment, (a) tax breaks and privileges for high earning individuals (e.g. on pensions and capital gains) would no longer be justified in terms of any supposed incentive to invest risk capital; (b) any squeezing of profits and consequent run-down in asset values would not damage the real economy – although it would of course be very negative for stock markets.

• Rapid *phasing out of tax havens* with a view to raising the tax take from corporate and other tax avoiders.

A compulsive hope

For a critical mass of the world's major nation-states even to arrive at the point where they would feel compelled to implement such a set of drastic measures obviously implies quite a dramatic Damascene conversion on the part of the ruling oligarchies concerned. As of mid-2009, such a possibility may well seem remote, especially given the balance of forces in the United States, where – notwithstanding the apparent popular desire for change expressed in the convincing victory of President Obama in 2008 – powerful reactionary forces still hold sway in both Washington and the corporate media. Hence it remains all too plausible to imagine that the US government, still deeply in thrall to big business, will continue to steer a desperate collision course with the forces of ineluctable change.

As against this there appears now to be a gathering recognition – even among mainstream economists – that the present economic model is permanently broken in at least one crucial respect: that it cannot – at least in the foreseeable future – possibly deliver a revival of growth on a sufficient scale to avert the financial and social disaster precipitated by the credit crunch of 2007–08. Thus one leading analyst has pointed out that, because US growth since the 1980s has been driven by credit-fuelled overconsumption and has also generated massive overinvestment in industries such as automobiles, 'it may not be feasible to reattain the growth levels in the global economy of the last twenty or so years'.[4] At the same time a British government agency has issued a report in 2009 pointing out that continued global growth at the pace recorded over the recent past (a fivefold increase in fifty years) will henceforth be unsustainable on ecological grounds, while recognising that the current economic system depends on its continuing.[5]

While these views hardly represent a consensus, they do indicate a new willingness on the part of officially respected analysts to question the whole basis of the existing growth-based model. It is therefore tempting to conclude that the self-evident truths

4. Satyajit Das, 'Built-to-Fail Economic Models', www.prudentbear.com; see also Chapter 2.

5. Professor Tim Jackson, *Prosperity without Growth? The Transition to a Sustainable Economy* (London: Sustainable Development Commission, 2009).

they are proclaiming will gradually gain a larger following and that this trend will prove irresistible once it becomes plain that the official recovery strategy is not only failing to achieve a return to meaningful growth but will turn out to be merely the prelude to an even more severe downturn than occurred in 2008. Yet such a relatively optimistic scenario reckons without the ruthless determination of the diehard vested interests in Wall Street, the City of London and elsewhere, who may well still feel they have nothing to lose by resisting, with the vast resources still at their disposal, any change that will threaten their own privileged position. Hence, as our collective plight becomes ever more desperate the fate of our species may hinge on whether those who have finally grasped the urgency of the need for radical change can provide the necessary leadership to take the world in that direction. Failing that, we may remain at the mercy of the perverted few who, like Hitler in his bunker in 1945, are prepared to bring down the world on top of themselves for the sake of prolonging their power to the bitter end.

Index

accountability, corporate, 119–20; democratic/political, 114, 154, 157, 160, 162, 167; *see also* corporate governance

accounting, false/'creative', 43–5 54, 58

actuarial profession, 44, 72n

advertising, 12, 52, 97, 154, 155

Afghanistan, 89, 168

Africa, 62, 88, 106, 115, 164

agricultural economics, perversion of, 57, 86–87

agriculture, 65, 85–6, 94, 106, 132

alienation, *see* labour

American Insurance Group (AIG), 22, 23

Anglo-Saxon countries, 72, 91, 118

Annan, Kofi (former UN secretary general), 105

anti-trust regulation, *see* monopoly

Argentina, 37n, 115

armaments industry, 5, 89

Asia, 2, 25, 39, 101, 106, 107, 114, 115, 163n

asset-backed securities (ABS), 21, 22, 23, 45

asset values, 45, 51, 171; in the context of privatisation, 66–7; inflation/manipulation of, 72

auditing/auditors, 20, 44

BAE Systems, 156

Bangladesh, 143

banking industry/sector, 12, 103, 118, 141, 143; bail-out of since 2007, 17, 34–7; failures, 41, 91; government underwriting/nationalisation, 36, 46, 166; lax regulation, 6, 26, 44–5; lobby, 44, 73; *see also* central banks, financial institutions

basic income, 124–7, 138, 139–40, 162

BBC (British Broadcasting Corporation), 62n, 154, 167n

Bernanke, Ben, 39

biotechnology, 53, 57, 98

Bolivia, 115

bonds/bond markets, 15, 39, 40, 57

Brandt Commission, 164

Britain 7 & n, 11, 32, 33, 34, 36, 60, 66, 69 & n, 80, 82, 88, 92, 101, 116, 118, 120, 122, 125, 127, 130, 137, 139, 142, 166, 167n; attack on Iraq in 2003, 111, 132; capital gains tax, 24; community